G000147473

Heavenly weddings
that don't cost the earth

Susan Sayers

First published in 2005 by
KEVIN MAYHEW LTD
Buxhall, Stowmarket, Suffolk, IP14 3BW
E-mail: info@kevinmayhewltd.com
www.kevinmayhew.com

© 2005 Susan Sayers

The right of Susan Sayers to be identified as the author of this work
has been asserted by her in accordance with the Copyright, Designs
and Patents Act 1988.

All rights reserved. No part of this publication may be reproduced,
stored in a retrieval system, or transmitted, in any form or by any
means, electronic, mechanical, photocopying, recording or otherwise,
without the prior written permission of the publisher.

Extracts from *Common Worship: Services and Prayers for the Church of
England* (on page 37) are copyright © The Archbishop's Council, 2000
and are produced by permission.

Bible quotations are from *The New Revised Standard Version* of the Bible
copyright 1989 by the Division of Christian Education of the National
Council of Churches in the USA, used by permission; the Holy Bible,
New International Version, copyright © 1973, 1978, 1984 by International
Bible Society. Used by permission of Hodder & Stoughton, a member
of the Hodder Headline Group. All rights reserved; *The Revised English
Bible* © Oxford University Press and Cambridge University Press 1989;
The Authorised (King James) Version. Rights in the Authorised Version
are vested in the Crown. Reproduced by permission of the Crown's
patentee, Cambridge University Press.

9 8 7 6 5 4 3 2 1 0

ISBN 1 84417 297 X
Catalogue No. 1500725

Cover design by Angela Selfe
Edited and typeset by Katherine Laidler

Printed and bound in Great Britain

Contents

With love and thanks to

Eleanor and Matt
Rachel and Alex

How this book came to be written

(Do ignore this bit unless you're wondering . . . !)

When I first considered getting married in the '60s I had this idea of a drifty, romantic meadow wedding in a village church, going out early in the morning to pick my wild flowers and everyone dancing to a live jazz band barefoot on the grass till dawn, ending with a swim in the sea.

That wedding didn't happen, and by the time I got married I was a convinced atheist, so it felt somehow false to get married in a church. By this time I wasn't into ceremonies of any kind, and our civic wedding was as basic, low-key and casual as possible, I think to mark up our chosen casual approach to marriage. It was just more convenient at that time, rather than simply living together, and we thought it quaint that some of our friends were still thinking of marriage in such an 'old-fashioned' way – with 'faithfulness' and 'lifelong' in the dream.

I remember us buying a wedding ring the day before, and my husband borrowing one of my dad's shirts. I had bought the shortest dress I could find, in pale blue broderie anglaise – just a pretty summer dress – and we had to borrow the fee from our friends during the wedding, as we'd forgotten about that.

Afterwards we had a nice meal in the garden which my mum had prepared, and then left in our old van to camp on the Yorkshire moors and have fun. I don't remember anyone taking any wedding photos; certainly we never had any ourselves.

That marriage lasted all of 18 months. Devastated and heart-broken and perhaps a little wiser, I gave up on the idea of marriage and concentrated on having as good (and largely irresponsible) a time as I could.

Then one day, and much to my embarrassment and reluctance, I discovered that God was a reality. Slowly – very slowly – I came to terms with the implications of this discovery for my own life and finally realised that there was no way I could ignore it. Eventually I gave up struggling against it and wearily said to God, 'OK. You win. I can see I need to get to know you better.'

I was walking alone on Ingleborough Hill in Yorkshire when that happened and I've rarely felt such relief and happiness and energy all at once. There I was dancing around on my way down the hill, grinning at the sheep like a lottery winner, and it all seemed so crazy and yet so obviously and deliciously right. When I got down to the village of Clapham I bought something to eat and drink, and had so much energy that I set off up the hill again. I couldn't bear to leave it just yet.

Usually when you read stories like this everything goes well afterwards, but I guess I'm not everyone. Not a great deal in my lifestyle changed at first. I certainly didn't start going to church straightaway or anything like that. But I was beginning to walk with Jesus and I'd started talking things over with him sometimes, when it suited me.

Then I met and moved in with the man who became my second husband, and this time we wanted to get married in the church I'd now started going to, making our vows in God's presence. Both of us wanted that. This time marriage was going to be for life, and I wanted to do it with prayers and a priest.

As I was divorced we were told it wasn't possible (this was in the '70s) and that hurt. They also suggested that perhaps we would consider stopping living together before getting married, and that I found offensive. What right had they to tell me how to live my life? The offer was there to have a marriage blessing following a civic ceremony, but I had all the memories of my previous civic ceremony and to me it seemed hypocritical of the church to be prepared to bless our marriage if they weren't prepared to marry us.

We found a church in the area willing to take the wedding, so we booked it for a few days before Christmas. My husband couldn't cope with anything more than the barest minimum of guests. A very few family members were invited to come. I wore a suit I already had and once again there were no photos. There was heavy snow and we went by taxi to the church from our home – after ringing around many taxi firms that morning. Afterwards my husband went to the pub for a drink with his brother-in-law while I came back to the house with my long-suffering mum and a couple of friends and cried into the gammon I'd cooked.

That marriage lasted nearly 20 years, and we have two lovely daughters, two wonderful sons-in-law and grandchildren.

After my own wedding days, I can't begin to tell you how much I've enjoyed those of our children! I never realised weddings could be such *fun*. It has been so exciting and joyous to be part of them that I was inspired to write this book, though at one time I would have thought it the very last thing I'd ever want to write about! I start getting all excited about your weddings, now, and wish you all the joy and happiness in the world.

Along the way I've been involved in many weddings of family and friends, intrigued by the different expectations and styles, and picked up ideas that seemed to work well for them. I've watched good marriages grow and blossom, and that's a real joy. And I've also been a listening ear as a friend and in my ministry as a priest to others whose marriages have been difficult or heartbreaking. Some of what I've learnt from the brave way people have worked through their problems is included here.

So I hope you enjoy reading it, and I hope it will give you the confidence to go for a heavenly wedding that doesn't cost the earth – either in money or stress!

SUSAN SAYERS

'We can't afford to get married'

So you'd like to get married and have a nice wedding? Suddenly it can look as if you'll be facing bankruptcy! Weddings have become so expensive that lots of couples put off getting married because they simply can't afford it. Or they equate 'church wedding' with 'expensive option' and assume only the wealthy can afford that luxury.

Well, it doesn't have to be like that. Relax. Heavenly weddings *don't* have to cost the earth! Somehow the lovely wedding traditions seem to have been turned into an extremely expensive kind of straitjacket that we all feel forced to wear. You don't have to get drawn into all that. Who wants to get married in a straitjacket?

This book is here to help you recover the freshness and fun of getting married in church as you'd like to, with a wonderful wedding you can enjoy to the full, along with as many or few guests as you like, but without that massive bill you can't afford.

There are plenty of ideas and information so you can choose the kind of wedding you want and still stay solvent. Or you can put all the money you save into your home. Or your honeymoon. It's up to you.

Weddings can be expensive in other ways, as well as financially. There can be quite unrealistic costs and expectations involving time, energy and family stress. Hopefully this book will help cut down on these costs too, so that your wedding doesn't get in the way of your marriage but actually gets your marriage off to a flying start.

So whether you choose to go for the traditional or the exotic, quiet or with a big crowd of well-wishers, putting together your own ceremony or following a regular 'service', your special day as a committed couple can celebrate your love and your new status in the community.

'We're getting married!'

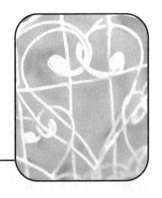

Perhaps you just knew – as soon as you first met – that you were right for each other. Perhaps it happened much more gradually over months or years, with friendship and shared experience deepening into love; or perhaps there's been all kinds of heart-searching along the way.

But there comes that moment when you both know that you need to be together for the rest of your life. In a strange way you know that being together will somehow allow you both to be more completely who you really are. It's a bit like a hug, where you hug and get hugged at the same time. You find you're being made happy and fulfilled while making your partner happy and fulfilled.

The person you are planning to marry may not be a movie star, but when it comes to being happy – you are. They're most probably not the media's stereotype of 'perfect' because, as we all know, that doesn't really exist, but they *are* perfect for you, which is the important thing, and very lovable. You love them very much, warts and all. You also know that you are accepted, valued and loved by the person who wants to marry you. You're perfect for them, and they love you, warts and all.

Some recent research suggests that being married often makes people both happier and more healthy, which is interesting. Not only is getting married tried and tested and still popular, it's now also officially good for you! We are often told about the number of marriages which fail and end in divorce, but that's often looking at the facts through the eyes of a pessimist. After all, if it's true that one in three marriages ends in divorce, that means that two out of every three marriages lasts and succeeds. That's quite a lot of marriages.

A working marriage is one of the best influences for good in any community. There's a relaxed happiness and trust which is infectious. There's a security and stability which spreads into the wider circle of friends and neighbours, affecting the way we all treat one another. Children grow up with their natural, instinctive enjoyment in life affirmed. Living in a committed loving partnership builds our confidence and allows us to blossom as human beings.

And it goes on often right into old age, with all those years of learning what loving and caring is all about, where the companion-ship of a marriage sustains each partner right to the end of their life. As grandparents and even great-grandparents, the extended family is blessed by the marriage commitment made so many years earlier. It's always touching to see an elderly couple walking together holding hands or sharing a joke. The love that you feel for one another now will last far beyond the colour of your hair or the smoothness of your skin. Love stays beautiful for ever.

Marriage – a public promise to be faithful for life – has been happening all over the planet in most cultures for thousands of years. In many ancient tribes the need was recognised for a secure place where children could be raised, and property and bloodline rights protected. In some cultures the marriage is arranged by the elders in a family, or by the parents, so that it is more about bind-ing whole families, rather than two people. Often marriage has been a kind of insurance policy against destitution in the event of widowhood.

Some marriages have been by proxy, with the couple only meeting up much later on, and at one time it was made illegal to be married after sunset – to cut down on the problem of brides being substituted and going unrecognised in the gloom! It's possible that the original 'ushers' were the bridegroom's private army who helped him raid and capture a bride from a different tribe, so as to keep the gene pool healthy. Lots of our wedding traditions have come down to us from quite ancient beliefs and tribal concerns.

So what about that special day when the marriage starts? Whether you've already been living together for years or are living separately until the wedding, the truth is that getting married is the start of something completely new. Marriage is something completely different from sharing the same home and making love.

Making those vows to one another in the presence of God and of your community changes not only both of you and your close family and friends, but the whole community. It's a kind of organic thing, and wonderful to celebrate in style.

But whose style? Don't be pressured into celebrating the making of your marriage in the way the media dictates. It's *your* marriage, after all! The way some people talk you'd think a wedding wasn't 'proper' without a particular assortment of traditions, but . . .

. . . **the most important ingredient of a wedding is two people who love each other enough to commit themselves to one another for the rest of their lives.**

And that is both the costliest item and the one that doesn't cost you a penny.

So really the whole essence of the marriage – with its years to come of deepening love and affection, perhaps a growing family and all those sleepless nights and magical milestones, with all the laughter and the tears, the shared life experiences of happiness and grief, the growing memories and friendships, the trust, faithfulness and mutual understanding, the mutual caring as you both grow old – all that is there in seed form at the wedding itself. Like I said, a marriage is organic.

It works the other way round as well. The actual wedding day of commitment and celebration is there throughout the whole of the marriage. How can that happen? Well, there are the pictures and recordings, of course, to remind you of how you started out, with the freshness and hopes and dreams, and the fashions all looking increasingly antique as the years go by, and youthful faces still just about recognisable!

Some couples choose to keep the wedding dress, dried bouquet or service sheet to bring out with the photos each year. And those wedding anniversaries *are* special and worth remembering, not only to celebrate but to reaffirm your committed love for one another. Sometimes at the 10-, 25- or 50-year anniversaries, people like to return to the place they were married and have a short service of renewing their marriage vows to one another before a party or celebration meal.

But it isn't just a yearly thing. On a daily basis the wedding feeds into the marriage, and it's here that the rings come into their own. Rings are an amazingly simple and beautiful symbol of your vows of eternal love, worn on your body all the time. Wedding rings through the ages have been made of bone or leather as well as silver or gold. The important thing about a ring is its continuous, all-the-way-around shape which is always there to remind you both, and the community, of your love union.

Hold your ring as you think of your partner and pray for them and your marriage day by day and year by year. Hold it whenever you need to forgive, or whenever you need courage to stay faithful. Healthy, strong marriages don't happen by accident –

they grow and need looking after carefully. The rings of your wedding day are a solid reminder of your promise and help you to care for your growing marriage so that it blossoms and fruits with happiness.

*A prayer to say each day
as you prepare for your wedding*

God of love
take our love and bless it.
May we always honour one another
with kindness and respect.
May we encourage one another
in all that is good
and most fully our true selves.
Amen.

Why get married in church?

A huge number of couples choose to have a church wedding, when it's perfectly possible to get married in any place which is registered for this legal contract. So why choose a church?

For many, a church just seems like the best possible setting for a wedding. It's traditional, putting us in touch with the brides and grooms from our family tree who through the generations have also got married in that context. The church buildings are often ancient and beautiful, and as we wear clothes from an earlier time in history, and celebrate an event which is making history for us, it feels right for this historic and special occasion to be acted out in a historical, traditional place. There's a sense of the present being rooted in the past, so that the past becomes a kind of blessing on the future.

And the fact that so much classical literature has the heroes and heroines celebrating their new life together in a church means that there is something particularly romantic about a church setting for a wedding. Think of some of those romantic weddings – Jane Eyre and Mr Rochester, Cinderella and the Prince, the double wedding of Elizabeth and Mr Darcy with her sister Jane and Mr Bingham, the marriage of Figaro, and of Romeo and Juliet.

But the most important, underlying reason for marrying in church is that you are making your vows of love and commitment to each other in the presence of the God of love. God's blessing is given to you both as you step out, husband and wife, into the future together. And many people, whether they regularly go to church or not, have a deep spiritual belief in God, and want this most special event to take place in a church, a house of God, a holy place where people have been saying their prayers for generations.

God has known and loved you both since before you were born. In one of the psalms you can hear the fondness and affection of God for each of us:

> For it was you who formed my inward parts;
> you knit me together in my mother's womb.
> I praise you, for I am fearfully and wonderfully made.
> Wonderful are your works; that I know very well.
> My frame was not hidden from you,
> when I was being made in secret,
> intricately woven in the depths of the earth.
> Your eyes beheld my unformed substance.
> In your book were written all the days
> that were formed for me,
> when none of them as yet existed.

Psalm 139:13-16 (New Revised Standard Version)

When each of my daughters was born I began praying for their husbands, should they marry. It wasn't that I was praying for husbands for them – that was nothing to do with me. But as I day-dreamed about them as adults it occurred to me that any husband they married was presumably growing up now, as they were, and the thought of these boys, whom I didn't know yet, one day becoming so important to the girls I so much loved, made me fond of them already, and I wanted to keep them in my prayers as they grew. It was a great privilege eventually to meet the people I'd been praying for over the years.

Why did I tell you that? Well, I suppose at each of my daughters' weddings, it helped bring home to me the way God's complete knowledge of us all is matched by his complete love for us, and God, who knows you both so well, has been watching the way both of you have been travelling towards this commitment. There's a great sense of thankfulness at a wedding that these two lives have journeyed, met and joined, with all the hope for a future life-partnership which blesses the whole community. A church wedding celebrates this to the full.

It may be that only one of you would feel comfortable saying you are a Christian – a follower of Jesus Christ – but out of love and respect for one another, one partner, who doesn't share the faith of the other, is more than happy to go along with something that means a great deal to the other. In most churches you are entitled to be married whether or not you have been christened – that means to have been baptised in the name of the Father and of the Son and of the Holy Spirit. However, the wedding service in all churches is Christian, and there are references all through it to Jesus Christ.

Some churches may suggest that as part of preparing for your marriage you join an Alpha group, marriage preparation or some other introductory course, in order to find out a bit more about the Christian faith and the God in whose presence you are making your solemn vows to each other. It may be suggested that if you have never been baptised, this is a good time to think seriously about that.

Even if this isn't offered, do ask any questions you have, and voice any of those concerns you have lurking in the back of your mind which make you uncomfortable with the idea of God. You may well find that the God you don't feel able to believe in is actually not believed in by the Church either. There are lots of widespread misunderstandings about the nature of God which point to a rather callous, cruel or impotent personality, light-years away from the God shown in the actual life of Jesus.

It is often at the life-changing times around a birth, a marriage or a death that people start asking the big questions about life and its meaning. So in case that includes you, I've included in this wedding book a chapter on the questions often asked about God and the Christian faith. And there are some suggestions for how you can find out more, if you're interested. You'll find all that starting on page 25.

If you haven't been in a church, chapel or cathedral recently, why not check one out together and just wander around. Use the short 'church guide' in the next chapter to help you make sense of what you find there, and pray the wedding preparation prayer on page 15, remembering that you are both well known to God already, and that he understands you and wants the very best for you both and all your loved ones.

Your church visit guide

Here are some of the things you can expect to find in a church, chapel or cathedral building. The church building is much more than a place for people to gather in, so you can pick up quite a lot about the Christian faith just by wandering round one.

A church is sometimes known as 'God's house', which suggests a spiritual presence of God living there. People talk with God and listen to his words when they are here. They worship, thank and praise God. All this makes the church a holy place, set apart for getting in touch with your soul and responding to God's love.

In the world of nature, you need to be quiet and still, and often patient if you want to see any wildlife. In rather the same way we need to wait on God expectantly in quietness and humility if we want to sense his presence. God is Spirit, so we won't be able to see him here with our physical eyes. But in stillness we may well sense God's presence, feel his peace and know his love for us.

Look at
the shape
of the church.
Often it is roughly built in the shape of a cross,
so that when
people gather here
they are actually
gathering together
inside a cross.

Why? At a particular date, just over 2000 years ago, a well-documented Jewish person called Jesus was born in the Middle East. Christians believe that the God who made us and the world was entering the world himself, as a human baby, as Jesus, the Son of God. When Jesus grew up he travelled around teaching people about God's kingdom of love, healing the sick and gathering in the outcasts of society. Jesus showed what God is really like, spoken in the language of a human life.

His honesty, mercy and love were too challenging, even for some of those who had been waiting for this very thing to happen, and Jesus was brought to trial by the religious leaders of the time and executed by Roman crucifixion. He went on loving and forgiving right through to death, showing us the full extent of God's love for us. On the third day after his death his body had gone from the tomb and he was seen by many people, alive again, but in a new dimension of life. Death could not hold the Lord of life.

In the cross shape of a church, and in every cross inside it, Christians celebrate the love Jesus showed by dying for us, and also their happiness that Jesus, once completely dead, is alive for ever.

The font or **baptistery** is a bath where those wanting to commit their lives to following Jesus Christ are christened (baptised) with water and God's Holy Spirit.

The altar or **Holy Table** is where Christians celebrate a meal together. At the last supper Jesus ate with his disciples before his death, he broke some bread and shared some wine. Speaking of his coming death he said, 'This is my body, broken for you. This is my blood, poured out for you and for many, for the forgiveness of sins.' He told his disciples that whenever they broke bread and shared wine together like this in his name, they would be in his presence.

The lectern is a reading desk, and it's here that the Holy Bible is read. It's also often from here that the preacher teaches people about God.

The Holy Bible is actually not one book but a library of ancient scrolls, dating from several thousands of years ago up to a couple of hundred years after Jesus lived on earth. They tell the story of God's love from creation through the lives of people like Abraham, Moses and the prophets, through the waiting for God's promised Christ (Messiah), to four different biographies of Jesus (Gospels), and the diaries and letters of the early Church.

Christians call the book holy because they believe it is inspired by God, and that God speaks to his people in every generation as they read it. Some of the books in this library are guide books and manuals, some poetry and drama, some journals and visions, some letters and fragments of distance learning courses, some biographical accounts of Jesus' life and teaching.

Stained glass windows are sometimes examples of the way people have told the stories of the Bible in pictures. Or they may show symbolic pictures of various followers of Christ whom Christians have found inspiring over the years, often known as saints. Coloured glass allows the sun's light to shine through, much as God's light shines through good and loving lives.

Candles are often found in churches, and people will light a candle as they pray for a person or a situation. Candles are a sign of Jesus, the Light of the World, shining in the darkness of pain and evil, always feeling for those who suffer, and transforming even the worst situations into places where healing and hope can be born.

Stations of the Cross are placed around the walls of some churches so that either alone or in a group you can walk as a pilgrim without travelling to Jerusalem, following the last journey Jesus took to his death.

Cushions may be provided for the comfort of those wanting to get down on their knees to pray in humility and love in the presence of Almighty God. There are many instances in the Bible where people, overwhelmed with the love and holiness of God, have found their knees giving way as they worship him.

Flowers of God's good creation are often brought in to remind people of God's blessings and goodness, and to celebrate this world of variety, colour, texture and shape.

The letters 'IHS' are sometimes found in the cloths and carvings in churches. They are the first three letters of the Greek spelling of JESUS, and traditionally Christians have added that they are the initials of what Jesus did for us: 'I Have Saved'.

The sign of a fish may be spotted too. This was the secret sign of early Christians when it was dangerous to be known as a believer. The Greek letters in the word for fish, *Ichthus*, made a kind of shorthand for 'Jesus Christ, God's Son, Saviour'. People of faith, including Christians, are still persecuted and imprisoned in some places today. Organisations like Amnesty International and Christian Aid can provide details and help with letter writing for those wanting to help in a practical way.

The Ten Commandments are displayed on the walls of some ancient churches. These are recorded in the Book of Exodus in the Bible, in chapter 20. Moses was given these laws for the people of Israel after they had walked to freedom from slavery in Egypt and were on their way to the Promised Land. These laws still hold good. Jesus summarised them as 'Love the Lord your God with all your heart and soul and mind and strength. And love your neighbour as yourself.'

Questions often asked about the Christian faith

There has to be a beginning somewhere – so who made God?

As humans and time-dwellers, we are used to a world of beginnings and endings. So we expect God to be the same. But God is not tied into the time thing like us – God inhabits eternity, where there aren't beginnings and ends. God always was, God is now and God always will be. Once we're outside the time zone ourselves (at death) we'll understand it easily.

If God is good and loving, why does he let all the terrible suffering happen?

Good question. You'd think that the good God of love would be rushing about stopping all the suffering wouldn't you? Because suffering hurts us so much it's really difficult to imagine why God doesn't keep intervening. We know from the Gospel biographies of Jesus that he reached out in compassion and love to those who suffered. We know God was prepared to come in person to share the terrible suffering of human pain and evil, so it isn't that God doesn't care that we suffer – completely the opposite.

It's more that for some reason the universe has been created with suffering and evil like a terrible price tag. So what could possibly be worth a price tag like that? Only one thing: for love – responsive, freely chosen love – to be possible. For God it's so important for us to be free to love that he was prepared to step out of the power seat and choose being alongside us with love and compassion, instead of powerfully and regularly breaking his own rules of

25

nature and intervening, which would turn creation into a kind of huge puppet.

God works within the natural laws of creation and gives us the strength and love we need to handle the suffering, so that it can be transformed from something evil and destructive into a force for good. It's far from comfortable, but God shares in the pain and, if we can bear to let him, brings us inner healing.

Who was Jesus?

There's more historical evidence for the existence of Jesus of Nazareth than there is for the existence of Julius Caesar, so we know he was an actual person, living in Palestine 2000 years ago. He was a Jewish prophet and healer, attracting huge crowds and proclaiming that the time of God's everlasting kingdom (which all Jews had been waiting for) had arrived. Everything in his loving behaviour and authoritative teaching pointed to Jesus being the long-awaited Messiah or Christ ('God's anointed one'). The religious leaders decided he was a fraud, blaspheming by claiming that he was God's Son. And the Roman authorities wanted no would-be kings threatening their power, so Jesus was executed by Roman crucifixion – a cursed death, according to Jewish law. He was certified dead by the test of his blood and water already separate when they pierced his side, and he was buried. On the third day after his burial he was seen alive, and the burial tomb was empty.

Christians – followers of the Christ, or Messiah – believe that Jesus was and is indeed the Son of God.

If Jesus is alive now, why can't we see him?

When he came back to life Jesus was in a kind of fuller dimension than before. He would suddenly be there in a room with his friends, without coming through the door, or he'd be there one minute and wasn't there the next. Not like a ghost, because he ate and drank with them. Then once they had got used to the fact that Jesus could be with them all the time and they didn't need to actually see him with their eyes, he went out of their sight, into the heavenly dimension, for the last time. This, he said, was so that with him physically absent, he would be able to send his Spirit to be among and within each of his followers through all the generations to come. Even now, Christians find Jesus present with them when they break bread together and when they communicate with him in prayer. Some things are more real even than seeing.

Where is heaven?

Heaven is not so much a place as the dimension of God's presence, which we can tune into during this earthly life whenever we worship God and live his way of humility and love. After death, we are invited to live entirely in the dimension of heaven, where all that is good and honest, faithful, true and lovely is focused because of God's presence. How we respond to God's love during our lifetime prepares us for how we respond to the invitation at our physical death.

Where is hell?

Hell is not so much a place as a dimension of alienation and separation from God, sometimes glimpsed during this earthly life, and the inevitable lasting consequence of choosing to reject God's invitation to full life and forgiveness at our physical death.

What happens when we die?

No human has come back from death to tell us what happens – except Jesus Christ. Jesus' life and teaching tell us that this earthbound life is not the whole story. We're not annihilated just because our physical body stops functioning. Love is stronger than death, and in a way our death is like a birth into the next stage of our life. In the womb we were in that safe, small environment with only the muted light and sounds of the big wide world outside. We couldn't imagine what it was like until we got out into its light, space and freedom. Whatever the post-death environment is like, it will be life in a whole new dimension.

Wasn't it cruel of God to send his Son into the world to die?

I sometimes think this is an unfortunate way of describing what happened, because it can sound as if God was doing the unthinkable as a parent. But when Jesus was born into this human existence, he was the expression of God's love. So God was there in the manger and on the cross. Jesus said, 'I am in the Father and the Father in me.'

How do you pray?

Praying is having a personal relationship with God, a two-way communication. Sometimes you can use words, sometimes you can just be conscious of being in God's company. You can use the words of other people in traditional prayers or just chat things over with God.

How does God get in touch with us?

God made us so he knows us completely and is much closer than having to speak through our ears. He speaks directly into our minds and hearts, or through the words we read in the Bible, or through events in our lives that he uses as a kind of picture language to teach us, or through one another. We might even find ourselves being part of the answer to someone else's prayer.

Why didn't God answer my prayer?

God always answers our prayers, but not necessarily in the way we'd like or the way we expect. God isn't like a slot machine or a Santa, there to provide our wish-list. It can hurt desperately when you pray for something close to your heart – like the recovery of a loved one – and what you pray for doesn't happen. God quite often says, 'No, but trust me – I'm bringing good out of this terrible situation,' and quite often, 'Not yet, be patient, there's a better time for this.' Often God will respond with an 'I'm afraid you're going to have to go through with this, and I know it's hard, but I promise to go through it with you and give you all the courage and support you need. Trust me. Hold on to me. We'll do it together.'

And quite often he responds immediately with a rush of love or peace of mind or a sudden brilliant idea that comes into our heads. That's for the times we ask God things, but a close relationship isn't all asking, of course. It's telling and listening and thanking and working on something together.

If Christians all believe in following Christ, why are there so many different churches?

Jesus prayed that his followers would stay united – like family – but instead we've had bad arguments over the centuries and split up, something we are trying to heal. Sometimes we do manage to work hard at valuing what we share, rather than focusing on what we understand differently. It's good to value our various different insights and to recognise that we are indeed like 'family' – united but with our own distinctive personalities. We're human and get it wrong, but thankfully God never gives up on us!

Questions often asked about weddings in church

Can we choose which church to get married in?

As a general rule you can get married either in a church in your local area where one of you lives or in the church you attend regularly, or are prepared to start attending. Marriage is a legal contract so these rules are to do with UK law.

If you have strong family connections with a particular church, you may still be able to get married there, even if it is not where you live. In all cases the church minister, pastor or priest will be able to give you more detailed information. (Their contact address, website or phone number is often displayed on the church notice boards or printed on the church newsletter.)

How long do you have to be in a place to be counted as a resident?

Your parish or district is where you have lived for at least two weeks prior to the wedding. The idea is that your marriage takes place in your own community.

Neither of us were christened. Does that matter?

This varies from church to church. To be married in a Roman Catholic church at least one of you needs to have been baptised as a Catholic, and the other would be expected to take part in a preparation course so that they are clear about the Christian faith. In Church of England, Methodist, Baptist and most other churches you do not need to have been baptised (christened) to be married.

31

We have been married before. Is this a problem?

All Christians hold that marriage, as taught by Christ, is for life, and the vows reflect this. It is also recognised that sometimes things go very wrong, and Christians believe in forgiveness, the wideness of God's mercy and the value of a fresh start. Trying to hold all that in proper balance isn't easy, and the Church is constantly wrestling with such tensions.

The Roman Catholic Church does not recognise divorce, and you can only get married again if your previous partner has died or if the previous marriage has been annulled. Your parish priest will be able to advise you further.

In Church of England, Methodist, Baptist, Salvation Army, Congregational and other Christian Churches more priests and ministers are now happy to marry those who have a divorced partner still living, depending on the circumstances. They would all expect to talk things through with you thoroughly, and by law certificates of divorce must always be produced before the marriage can take place.

Those pastors and priests unwilling to marry divorced people in church are very often happy to offer a service of prayer and dedication following a secular registration of remarriage.

I've heard of divorced and remarried people having a church blessing. Is this a kind of wedding?

A church blessing is a service of prayer and dedication following a civil marriage that takes place at a register office or place approved for civil marriage. This services commits the marriage promises to God's love and protection and celebrates the recently joined lives in God's presence. The couple may remind themselves of the vows they have taken by repeating them in this service.

Since the legal contract has already been made elsewhere, banns of marriage are not necessary, and neither is any entry made in the Register of Marriages.

Whereas a marriage can only take place in a registered, licensed building, a service of prayer and dedication can take place any-where, inside or outside.

We have both been widowed. Can we have prayers referring to our previous happy marriages at this new marriage?

Certainly. There is opportunity in the prayers to include anyone you especially want mentioned. Some couples may like to light a candle at some point in the service to remember the spouse who has died. Talk this over with the minister or priest who will be able to help you make the service reflect your thinking and feelings.

Can we choose our hymns and readings?

Obviously the minister taking the service has the last word on what is said and sung at any service, but in practice it's something for you all to plan together. Some churches have set words and others don't, but in all cases there is the possibility for designing the service to reflect your particular character. There are suggestions for hymns and music on page 57.

What are banns of marriage?

A wedding is a legal as well as a religious ceremony, and by law the intention of the couple to get married has to be made public prior to the marriage, so that full opportunity is given to raise objections. In a civil ceremony the notices of marriage are displayed on the notice board at the register office. In the Church of England where the minister is also the official registrar, banns giving notice of the marriage have to be read out at the main Sunday service for three consecutive weeks, at some point during the three months before the wedding.

Where are the banns of marriage called?

At the church of the parish in which each partner lives, and at the church where the wedding will take place. If either partner is a member of another church, the banns must be read there as well. So sometimes this will involve only one church and sometimes more. Often the minister or priest will follow the reading of the banns with a prayer for those preparing to get married, so that you are being supported in prayer by the whole local church community. Many of them will be remembering you in their daily prayers as well. In some circumstances a common or special licence may be necessary. The minister will be able to advise you about this.

How do we book a church for our wedding?

As early as possible, and certainly before you book any reception venue, get in touch with the minister or priest at the church where you are hoping to get married, to check that the church and the minister are available for the date you want and to discuss your wedding plans. Leave plenty of time to sort out all the legal requirements.

Can we have photos and video taken during the wedding?

Usually there is no objection, unless it's likely to be intrusive and interrupt the service. It's important for those taking pictures to be sensitive to the feelings of everyone concerned, and as discreet as possible.

How old do you have to be to get married?

You must both be over the age of 16 years. If you are younger than 18 years you will need written permission from your parents or legal guardians. There is no upper age limit.

Does the bride have to be 'given away'?

No, she doesn't. This is an entirely optional traditional ceremony. If you want to include it, the bride's father, mother, or other person representing the family, gives the bride's right hand to the minister who places it in the hand of the bridegroom.

There is an alternative, newer tradition of both sets of parents being asked something like, 'Will you now entrust your son and daughter to one another as they come to be married?' to which they reply, 'We will.'

Does the bride have to promise to obey her husband?

No. This is optional. There are several possible forms of the vows and declaration for you to choose from.

Can we go into the church together, instead of separately?

Yes.

Can we invite a minister of another Christian Church to take part in the wedding ceremony?

Obviously you will need to talk about this with the minister of the church where you are getting married, but there is not usually a problem. Certain parts of the service may have to be led by the church minister, but others can lead the rest of the ceremony.

What is the smallest number of people necessary for a marriage ceremony?

There only needs to be five people present for a marriage ceremony. These are the bride and bridegroom, the minister or registrar, and two witnesses.

The marriage service

What is a Christian wedding service like? Whatever the church tradition, at the heart of the marriage service are the promises which the bride and bridegroom make to each other in the presence of God and the couple's family and friends. Although these will vary slightly from church to church, they all reflect the same love and commitment through all circumstances, recognising the importance of cherishing and respecting one another and of faithfulness in the marriage. They celebrate your love and ask God's blessing on your life together.

The usual pattern is that the bridegroom and guests are already present and then the bride comes in, walking up to the front of the church where she stands with the bridegroom. The minister or priest will welcome everyone and say a few words about why we are all here, there may be hymns, prayers and readings, music, a talk, and then those special promises – the marriage vows.

As these vows are so important, there is often a question and answer conversation first between the bride, bridegroom and pastor.

Here, for instance, is the Church of England version of that:

> *Stuart*, will you take *Catherine* to be your wife? Will you love her, comfort her, honour and protect her, and forsaking all others, be faithful to her as long as you both shall live?
>
> I will.

Catherine, will you take *Stuart* to be your husband? Will you love him, comfort him, honour and protect him, and forsaking all others, be faithful to him as long as you both shall live?

I will.

Now that it's absolutely clear there are no legal objections to the marriage, and the bride and groom are both happy to make the vows to each other, the promises can go ahead.

You don't need to worry about learning them off by heart and forgetting them completely in the emotions of the moment, because the minister or priest will practise with you beforehand and say each phrase for you to repeat, all the way through the promises. And here they are. I've set them out as the short phrases will be said:

I, *Stuart*, take you, *Catherine*,
to be my wife,
to have and to hold
from this day forward;
for better, for worse,
for richer, for poorer,
in sickness and in health,
to love and to cherish,
till death us do part;
according to God's holy law.
In the presence of God I make this vow.

I, *Catherine*, take you, *Stuart*,
to be my husband,
to have and to hold
from this day forward;
for better, for worse,
for richer, for poorer,
in sickness and in health,
to love and to cherish,

till death us do part;
according to God's holy law.
In the presence of God I make this vow.

You hold each other's hand during your promises, and because you don't have to read anything you can look lovingly at one another as you commit yourself to each other.

Rings are usually given, and there will be prayers of blessing for the just-marrieds and their families.

The registers are signed and then the bride and bridegroom lead the procession down the aisle and out into their new life together.

The real cost of a wedding

The cost of a wedding with all the trimmings across the UK can be massive – with an average of £16,500, and many weddings costing nearer £20,000!

With such a huge bill, no wonder the months leading up to the wedding, and recovering financially afterwards, can be fraught with the extra, unnecessary expense of tension and stress. There must be a better way!

Change your thinking

Think of a wedding differently, and suddenly that bill can be cut down to between £1000 and £3000. If you want to go for the beauty of complete simplicity, you can be looking at no more than £500 for everything – that's only £250 each.

The cost of the legal fees in the Church of England, for instance, is just over £200:

£18 for the reading of the banns of marriage

£198 for the registration in church by a licensed minister

£3.50 for a Marriage Certificate issued on the day

When you consider that this is a life-changing legal registration involving two people, just over £100 each is not all that expensive.

41

The subtle take-over bid

One reason for the high expense is in that word 'professional'. It's a word that sounds good and worthwhile, but I think there's a real downside to it. Because we're all entertained and informed by professionals on the TV in the heart of our living rooms, the danger is that we have become subtly de-skilled, measuring up all our homegrown expertise against the high (or perhaps just slick) standards we see every day and perceive as 'local'. That can have the very negative effect of making us dissatisfied with anything which hasn't got that shiny 'professional' look to it, and discouraged from having a go ourselves.

It's rather like the way we prefer to buy 'professional' uniformly shaped fruit and vegetables, even though our locally produced, homegrown, differently shaped ones may well taste far better and be much fresher.

Why should the professionals have all the fun?

I think we need to rebel! Let's stand up to this eroding of local and homegrown confidence, and start valuing things slightly differently. For instance . . . flowers, grown, picked or chosen thoughtfully and arranged with love are surely more beautiful than the professional package deal of exact precision. Whatever madness persuaded us to see a clinical type of arrangement as superior for a wedding?

And another thing. Most people own good digital cameras these days. Many of them are talented at taking pictures. Computers make it easy to adjust and play around with images. So why do we still feel pressured to buy in the professional photographers, who can sometimes be unnecessarily intrusive and overbearing? We could equally well encourage some of our own friends and family, setting them up with disposable cameras, sharing their phone and digital camera images and having a more natural and varied set of pictures to remember the day. They'll be different from the professional photographer look, of course, but certainly not inferior. There's likely to be a fresher, more vibrant feel to them, with lots more character.

What's true for flowers and photographs is also true for bridal wear, transport, venue, catering, music, stationery and honeymoon. We can reclaim the ground that has been taken from us, so that the important events of our lives, like weddings, become celebrations we can enjoy being involved in ourselves, rather than forking out for the professionals to have all the fun!

Valuable by-products

When our involvement in our own wedding is limited to the worry and planning and paying, we also miss out on some of the lovely, long-lasting by-products of a wedding without so many professionals. For a start, our own part in the event changes. Instead of being in the role of celebrities, wheeled on to the stage of someone else's production, the whole event becomes ours – we can own it in a more satisfying and fulfilling way.

But there's more. Getting married is very much a whole family event – which affects the community. And if the celebrations of the wedding day grow out of that, with lots of involvement from family and friends, all using their skills and gifts as part of the festivity, the whole marriage, the whole family and the whole community will be enriched. There's a bonding and team spirit which helps us all become more of a healthy community as a result of working together to celebrate such a joyful event. This is a generosity which grows from our love and friendship with those starting out on their new life together.

It's always costly to have a celebration, but this way the giving and receiving happen at the same time, with those who are giving of their time and skills and energy also on the receiving end. The whole community gives to the bride and groom, who in turn are giving to the community. Everyone wins, and the costs are kept down because no one's out to make a living from it. We're all in it together for our own collective benefit.

In the next few chapters we'll take a fresh look at some of the main areas of expense in a traditional church wedding and see how they can be approached in alternative and creative ways which are far less expensive and more satisfying. They're just ideas to get you thinking – you may well find yourself suddenly imagining loads of other ways to do these things. All you needed was the permission and the confidence to let your imagination fly free. Enjoy.

The wedding clothes

For the bride

Received wisdom tells us that the bride's dress has to be the most expensive possible, never worn by anyone before, a 'dream' of a dress which turns the bride into a princess for the day. It has to be white and fairly impractical, so as to underline the 'special, fairy-tale day' factor.

Now let's look at that slightly differently. Received wisdom tells us that the bride is coming to church to make her vows of marriage to the man she loves, and receive his vows of marriage to her. She has chosen for this to happen not only in the presence of her family and community of friends and colleagues but also in the presence of the God of love. What she wears will reflect who she is and the sense that this marriage service is a symbol of their whole loving lifetime together as one.

You can see that the choice of dress for the bride really starts in the understanding and perception of what she is doing while wearing it. Making vows about a lifelong commitment is both serious and exciting, both full of celebration and also full of a practical reality. This isn't actually performance or dreamland at all. It's for real. It's amazing. It's special and holy.

So how does that affect our thinking about the dress?

Maybe it allows you to think beyond what the wedding magazines might prescribe, and beyond those unrealistically expensive expectations many people have. Perhaps the bridal dress just needs to be beautiful, suiting the bride stunningly, and reflecting both the solemnity and festive joy of the occasion?

If that's the case, then somehow the pressure is off, and you can relax as you choose your dress.

Making your own dress (with a little help from your friends) is not as impossible as you may think. Dressmaking is only scary because we've all got out of the habit of doing it. You can have exactly the fabric you want, too. You could even knit yourself a lacy dress. Patterns are much easier to follow than they once were, and you can choose one fitted to the level of your ability – some are particularly suitable for those with little experience. If you are using your wedding dress to learn the skills, your dress will have given you lifelong wear and practical usefulness!

Making your own dress also belongs to a much older tradition than the flouncy bought model, for that very reason – the bride was learning a craft that would be invaluable during her married life. A woman was known as a 'spinster' while spinning the yarn for making her wedding dress, becoming a 'wife' when she was married and had 'woven' the cloth.

Here are a few hints and ideas:

- Buy, or borrow from the library, a few basic books on dress-making to help you and give you confidence.
- Choose a simple design (it doesn't have to be specifically a wedding design – evening or party dresses made in white can become wedding dresses). Sometimes patterns come free with magazines.
- Go for gorgeous fabric.
- Consider a trip to somewhere exotic for a holiday, stay in local accommodation to aid their economy and buy material there, very cheaply and full of holiday memories. Sari lengths are excellent, or Chinese silk, for instance.
- Alternatively, visit an sari shop in your area and buy your fabric there. (In the London area, for instance, Shepherd's Bush is

excellent.) Browse in your local market – or travel to a market well known for cheap fabric of good quality. Look at curtaining material as well – don't assume the best wedding dress fabric will necessarily be in the highly priced and specialised wedding departments.

- It's helpful to use a dressmaker's dummy for fitting at each stage and storing your dress while you work on it. (Borrow or buy one secondhand.)
- Get together with a couple of friends and help one another along with the work so your dress comes out of quality time spent with friends or family.
- Enrol on a local dressmaking course and make the dress as your project there, with supervision and help from a professional.
- Start in good time so you don't have to rush it.

What about buying a dress?

- Go on a visit to somewhere like Thailand, Vietnam or China where you can have a wonderful break, meet the locals, and your dress can be skilfully made for you with fabric of your choice. Allow several days for the making. (Bring with you the measurements of the bridegroom and best man, and their suits can be made for you as well.)
- Buy on eBay.
- Browse the 'for sale' pages of the local paper for secondhand bargains.
- Buy when there's a sale on.
- Wear clothes you have already bought and love wearing. Add flowers and colour-coordinated shoes and you'll look lovely in clothes which will continue to remind you of your special day whenever you wear them.

For the bridegroom

Once again, the choices begin with our understanding of what we are doing at this wedding event. If it's a dressing-up costume drama we're acting in, then the hiring of tuxedos becomes vital. If, on the other hand, the celebration of love and commitment vows is of most importance, the dress code is suddenly more flexible and practical.

- Now is the time to visit somewhere in the world where tailoring still happens in the market place. Bring the measurements and have matching suits to own, made up beautifully for less than it costs to hire them for a day. This kind of tourism is much appreciated by locals as your money goes directly to them and you gain in having real contact with a different culture. Why not send a wedding picture to the maker of your suit?
- For a retro look, browse the charity shops.
- Look round the best street markets – travel to another city for the day.
- Buy on eBay.
- Wear a smart suit you already own, buy a special shirt and tie, and new or well-cared-for shoes. You'll feel yourself, confident and comfortable.

For the bridesmaids

- Once again, consider visiting another country such as Vietnam, Thailand or India, or one of the African or South American countries where public dressmakers are still widespread and part of everyday life. Support their economy and tourist industry by staying in local hotels and buying the fabric and/or having the dresses made up while you're there. Shoes can also be bought there and dyed to match, or be made up in the same fabric.
- Think about choosing a pattern suited to their skills and asking bridesmaids' families to provide the dress as their wedding gift.

- Each bridesmaid chooses a favourite dress she already owns and wears that, with flowers in her hair and a small bunch of fresh flowers to carry.
- Look for a pretty dress which all bridesmaids like and buy the same model in different sizes.
- Buy dresses in the same design but different colours.

For the pageboys
- A new shirt and smart pair of trousers – as for any important party celebration.

The wedding flowers

Wedding flowers are quite an expensive item if you have them professionally done, but relatively inexpensive if you do them 'in house', even if you use plenty of beautiful, quality flowers.

But, more importantly, doing the flowers for a bride and groom you love is one of the loveliest wedding presents. I have done the flowers for the weddings of both of my daughters, and it was so special to choose flowers and herbs with their particular personalities in mind.

My mother used to say that love was the ingredient that made her cooking taste so good and, although I'm no cook, I understood what she meant as I lovingly chose, prepared and assembled my floral 'ingredients'. And I had taught myself the skills, practising in the garden with bunches of rather jaded special offers from the supermarket every week until I got the hang of it.

Flower-arranging classes are often available locally, and flower-arranging groups often advertise demonstration sessions which are valuable. Watching someone actually creating an arrangement in front of your eyes helps you understand some of those diagrams in the teaching books.

All it takes is a bit of confidence to train yourself in a new skill, and anyone who is reasonably good at arts and crafts can learn enough basic floristry to create a bouquet for the bride, posies for the bridesmaids, flowers for the hair and buttonholes.

Floral arrangements for the church and tabletop arrangements for the reception are not at all difficult provided you're happy to learn the principles and have some practice sessions in the months leading up to the wedding.

By far the friendliest and most fun way of working is to have a small mixed-age group of family members and friends who get together and encourage each other. Even beginners can copy a tiny table design, for instance, so a group of you can complete the reception flowers quite quickly.

I found the buttonholes quite fiddly at first, and once again you will need to put in some practice. You don't need expensive flowers for the practice runs, though. Once you get the hang of it, you can get more imaginative too.

Learning the skills

You can buy clearly written guides to flower arranging for weddings, but you probably won't need to. Libraries carry excellent stocks of such books, so have a browse and read through several. You'll find you're picking up useful principles almost without noticing.

Go for books with plenty of pictures and diagrams. Not only are they easier to learn from but also they'll get you thinking creatively and imaginatively about flower possibilities, so you'll be more confident to experiment and adapt to make your flower arranging personal. Make use of any local demonstration classes and ask advice from those who have been 'doing the flowers' for years.

Look around the bouquets of flowers sold in the supermarkets, and around florist shops, garden centres and market stalls, noticing the different flowers available and which go well together. Notice the flowers and greenery in the gardens of family and friends, and ask if they'd mind you having some to practise with, and on the day.

Equipment you'll need

- Space – outside is ideal.
- Buckets and bowls to store your flowers and keep them fresh.
- Water sprayer and watering can.

- Scissors, knife and secateurs.
- Gardening gloves for handling prickly plants as you rid them of thorns and prickles.
- Dustpan and brush, broom and black plastic bags for protecting the floor and clearing up.
- Raffia and garden twine to bind flowers together.
- Florists' wire, which comes in different thicknesses and types according to use.
- Blocks of 'oasis' foam which hold water and support the flowers in your arrangement.
- Florists' waterproof tape.
- Containers for flower arrangements.
- Cardboard boxes, tissue paper and plastic bags for keeping corsages fresh once assembled.
- Music, friends and refreshments!

You will, of course, find more detailed lists in specialist books, but this list is here to show you how *ordinary* most of the items are – which hopefully will encourage you. Don't let the scary Wedding Monster put you off trying something which is such fun and so satisfying!

The wedding pictures

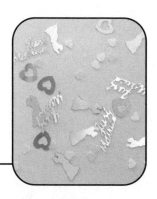

Here's another professional spend item on which you can easily save money by doing the pictures 'in house'. Which means you can also dispense with the slightly outdated formality of regimented wedding photos and photos taking longer than the wedding itself.

Especially now that many more people have digital cameras which take good quality pictures, you can invite people to bring their cameras and share the pictures taken. Digital cameras have revolutionised our attitude to photography. We can take pictures in far greater quantity and then select our favourites to print. That way there's more chance of catching the real buzz of the wedding atmosphere. And as we can now play with our images on screen, zooming in, adjusting the brightness and so on, you can gather a collection of pictures by your amateur friends and family which will make a stunning wedding album.

- Consider asking for wedding photos, video or a compiled wedding album as a wedding gift.
- Encourage people to bring their cameras and share the images.
- Consider buying a number of single-use cameras and giving them out to people so you get images from many different viewpoints.
- Beforehand write out large signs of who you want in each of the main photo shoots and ask a friend to display them one by one so no one has to bellow.

The wedding music

Old William Dewy, with the violincello, played the bass; his grandson Dick the treble violin; and Reuben and Michael Mail the tenor and second violins respectively . . . 'Times have changed from the times they used to be,' said Mail . . . 'People don't care much about us now! I've been thinking we must be almost the last left in the county of the old string players? Barrel-organs, and the things next door to 'em that you blow wi' your foot, have come in terribly of late years' . . .

'More's the pity,' replied another. 'Time was – long and merry ago now! – when not one of the varmits was to be heard of; but it served some of the quires right. They should have stuck to strings as we did, and kept out clarinets, and done away with serpents. If you'd thrive in musical religion, stick to strings, says I.'

Thomas Hardy 'Going the Rounds',
Under the Greenwood Tree (1872)

The choice of music is much wider than you'd think – it's just that so many choose the same wedding pieces, that we tend to think of a wedding being incomplete without the 'wedding march'. Just in case you feel like broadening your choice of music a little, I'm giving you a list including some less usual pieces of music for you to consider, all of them lovely and well worth a listen, even if you do decide on one of the traditional wedding marches at the end of your musical cruise.

The following are very popular for going in and coming out of church:

- *Arrival of the Queen of Sheba*, Handel
- *Trumpet Voluntary*, Clarke
- *Wedding March*, Mendelssohn
- *Bridal March*, Wagner
- *Trumpet Tune and Air*, Purcell
- *Pomp and Circumstance No. 4 in G*, Elgar
- *Toccata*, Widor

Or try something used less often but just as beautiful and appropriate:

- *1812 Overture*, Tchaikovsky
- 'Ode to Joy' from *Symphony No. 9*, Beethoven
- Overture to *Music for the Royal Fireworks*, Handel
- 'The Ball' from *Romeo and Juliet*, Prokofiev
- Intermezzo from *Cavalleria Rusticana*, Mascagni
- 'Pas d'Action' from *Swan Lake*, Tchaikovsky
- 'Spring' from *The Four Seasons*, Vivaldi
- *Sarabande*, Handel
- *Canon*, Pachelbel
- *The Swan*, Saint-Saëns
- March from *Aida*, Verdi

You could try tuning in to a music radio station such as Classic FM sometimes, to hear a wide range of classical music – if you hear something you really like and miss the title, you can always find out what it was by phoning in to them or logging on to their website. I've sometimes sat out in my car after I've parked at home, spellbound by some amazing music I've never heard before and wanting to hear it through to the announcement.

At many churches you can book an organist for around £50, who will play suitable music before and after the service, during the signing of the register and for any hymns.

Alternatively you can use recorded music, either instead of the organ or to complement it. Many churches have sound systems to play tracks from tapes or CDs. If your church doesn't have that facility, ask if you can bring your own, and enlist a friend who knows the CD player well to be in charge of it. Write in the CD title and track number clearly on the service sheet for your sound manager, so they're in no doubt about when to switch on and off, and ask them to practise beforehand.

If you choose this option you're free to have whatever instruments and style you want, within reason. If you have musicians among your family and friends, think about including them in the service. Their playing could be their gift to you. Or students from a local music school or college may be interested in playing for you. Discuss your choices with the pastor, minister or priest, so you can come to a common understanding.

There are CDs available now of organ or music group accompaniment for hymns, so you don't have to bypass hymns even if you aren't having an organist. (*No organist? No problem!*, *No music group? No problem!*, *No pianist? No problem!* and *Favourite Wedding Music* are all available from Kevin Mayhew.)

Hymns

When it comes to wedding hymns, people are often rather stuck. Unless you go regularly to church you won't be familiar with the huge variety of hymns which have appeared over recent years, and you may only know a couple of things you sang at school. I imagine that's partly why 'All things bright and beautiful' and 'Give me joy in my heart' are so frequently chosen as wedding hymns.

Well, there are some beautiful hymns which are lovely to sing at a wedding – some of them ancient melodies which have been sung at weddings through the centuries, some which are contemporary and manage to express what all of us at the celebration feel in our hearts and would like to say. In that respect, hymns are a bit like the words in greetings cards – yes, sometimes they're shallow and sentimental and won't do at all, but sometimes we choose a hymn or a card because the words seem particularly apt and sensitive.

I was trying to work out how to bridge the gap for those of you who might not know many hymns but would be interested in having something sung at your wedding which really speaks to the bride and groom and everyone there. This is what I've come up with.

Some of the tunes will probably be familiar as they are traditional melodies. And I've included the words for some hymns which I think you might find specially appropriate. There is a useful website – www.cyberhymnal.org – where you can listen to MIDI files of many hymn tunes. So you can sit down with your hot chocolate or a whisky and try singing along the words with the tunes. *Then* make your choice of wedding hymns, from a far better informed position.

To the tune of 'Jerusalem'[1]

1 We gather here, we gather now,
   drawn by the love we know and share.
   We come to celebrate in our joy
   the union of this bridal pair.
   To them our hearts reach out with love.
   On them the light of heaven above
   shines down in grace abundant and free
   to bless them both eternally.

2 And we who join to wish them well
   offer them both our love and prayer,
   that they may walk in fullness of life
   the journey they have come to share;
   that they may know if storms come near
   that they have friends and family here,
   for we commit ourselves to pray
   and love and cherish them each day.

Words by Susan Sayers

---

[1] www.cyberhymnal.org/htm/j/e/r/jerusalem/htm

To the tune of 'Danny Boy'[1]

1 The love we share, the love we come to celebrate,
   so rich and full, so healing and so strong,
   comes from the love of God our loving Father,
   within whose care we all of us belong.
   A love which breathed creation into being,
   a love which knows what we can each become,
   a love which now within this marriage-making
   alights on bride and groom to bless and make them one.

2 Through future years, may they hold bright the memory
   of all the joys on this their wedding day.
   And as their love grows stronger yet and deeper,
   their rings express much more than words can say.
   They speak of love that never has an ending,
   of love that shines, encircles in embrace,
   of love whose heart is always free and open;
   our human love reflects the beauty of God's grace.

Words by Susan Sayers

Lord of all hopefulness

1 Lord of all hopefulness, Lord of all joy,
   whose trust, ever childlike,   no cares could destroy,
   be there at our waking, and give us, we pray,
   your bliss in our hearts, Lord, at the break of the day.

2 Lord of all eagerness, Lord of all faith,
   whose strong hands were skilled at the plane and the lathe,
   be there at our labours, and give us, we pray,
   your strength in our hearts, Lord, at the noon of the day.

---

[1] www.cyberhymnal.org/htm/m/o/modearla.htm

3 Lord of all kindliness, Lord of all grace,
   your hands swift to welcome, your arms to embrace,
   be there at our homing, and give us, we pray,
   your love in our hearts, Lord, at the eve of the day.

4 Lord of all gentleness, Lord of all balm,
   whose voice is contentment, whose presence is calm,
   be there at our sleeping, and give us, we pray,
   your peace in our hearts, Lord, at the end of the day.

Words by Jan Struther (1901–1953)
Used by permission of Oxford University Press

Praise, my soul, the King of heaven[1]

1 Praise, my soul, the King of heaven!
   To his feet thy tribute bring;
   ransomed, healed, restored, forgiven,
   who like me his praise should sing?
   Praise him! Praise him!
   Praise him! Praise him!
   Praise the everlasting King!

2 Praise him for his grace and favour
   to our fathers in distress;
   praise him still the same for ever,
   slow to chide and swift to bless.
   Praise him! Praise him!
   Praise him! Praise him!
   Glorious in his faithfulness!

3 Father-like he tends and spares us;
   well our feeble frame he knows;
   in his hands he gently bears us,
   rescues us from all our foes.

---

[1] www.cyberhymnal.org/htm/p/r/praisems.htm

Praise him! Praise him!
Praise him! Praise him!
Widely as his mercy flows!

4 Angels, help us to adore him;
ye behold him face to face;
sun and moon bow down before him,
dwellers all in time and space.
Praise him! Praise him!
Praise him! Praise him!
Praise with us the God of grace!

Words by Henry Francis Lyte (1793–1847)

Now thank we all our God[1]

1 Now thank we all our God,
with hearts and hands and voices,
who wondrous things hath done,
in whom his world rejoices;
who from our mother's arms
hath blessed us on our way
with countless gifts of love,
and still is ours today.

2 O may this bounteous God
through all our lives be near us,
with ever joyful hearts
and blessed peace to cheer us;
and keep us in his grace,
and guide us when perplexed,
and free us from all ills
in this world and the next.

---

[1] www.cyberhymnal.org/htm/n/o/nowthank.htm

3 All praise and thanks to God
   the Father now be given,
   the Son and him who reigns
   with them in highest heaven,
   the one eternal God,
   whom earth and heaven adore;
   for thus it was, is now,
   and shall be evermore.

Words by Martin Rinkart (1586–1649)
Translated by Catherine Winkworth (1827–1878)

Give me joy in my heart

1 Give me joy in my heart, keep me praising,
   give me joy in my heart, I pray.
   Give me joy in my heart, keep me praising,
   keep me praising till the end of day.

   Sing hosanna! Sing hosanna!
   Sing hosanna to the King of kings!
   Sing hosanna! Sing hosanna!
   Sing hosanna to the King!

2 Give me peace in my heart, keep me resting . . .

3 Give me love in my heart, keep me serving . . .

Words: Traditional

Morning has broken

1 Morning has broken like the first morning,
   blackbird has spoken like the first bird.
   Praise for the singing! Praise for the morning!
   Praise for them, springing fresh from the Word!

2 Sweet the rain's new fall, sunlit from heaven,
   like the first dew-fall on the first grass.
   Praise for the sweetness of the wet garden,
   sprung in completeness where his feet pass.

3 Mine is the sunlight! Mine is the morning
  born of the one light Eden saw play!
  Praise with elation, praise every morning,
  God's re-creation of the new day!

Words by Eleanor Farjeon (1881–1965)
© David Higham Associates. Used by permission from
The Children's Bells, published by Oxford University Press

To the tune of 'I vow to thee my country'[1]

1 These vows of love are taken, these rings of love received;
  we witness here among us a mystery believed:
  that in God's holy presence a marriage has begun
  and these your precious children have now become as one.
  For the things of earth and heaven draw closer as we pray
  and in heaven the angels celebrate with us on earth today.

2 For all our many blessings we offer thanks and praise,
  for gifts of love and fellowship our thankful hearts we raise.
  God's hand has held us safely and brought us to this day,
  God has guided and protected and taught us on the way,
  for the love we learn on earth is the love we'll find in heaven
  and the human love we celebrate is love that God has given.

Words by Susan Sayers

Lead us, heavenly Father, lead us[2]

1 Lead us, heavenly Father, lead us
  o'er the world's tempestuous sea;
  guard us, guide us, keep us, feed us,
  for we have no help but thee;
  yet possessing every blessing
  if our God our Father be.

---

[1] www.cyberhymnal.org/htm/i/v/ivow2the.htm
[2] www.cyberhymnal.org/htm/l/e/leadushf.htm

2 Saviour, breathe forgiveness o'er us,
   all our weakness thou dost know,
   thou didst tread this earth before us,
   thou didst feel its keenest woe;
   lone and dreary, faint and weary,
   through the desert thou didst go.

3 Spirit of our God, descending,
   fill our hearts with heavenly joy,
   love with every passion blending,
   pleasure that can never cloy;
   thus provided, pardoned, guided,
   nothing can our peace destroy.

Words by James Edmeston (1791–1867)

All things bright and beautiful

All things bright and beautiful,
all creatures great and small,
all things wise and wonderful,
the Lord God made them all.

1 Each little flow'r that opens,
   each little bird that sings,
   he made their glowing colours,
   he made their tiny wings.

2 The purple headed mountain,
   the river running by,
   the sunset and the morning
   that brightens up the sky.

3 The cold wind in the winter,
   the pleasant summer sun,
   the ripe fruits in the garden,
   he made them every one.

4 He gave us eyes to see them
  and lips that we might tell
  how great is God almighty
  who has made all things well.

Words by Cecil Frances Alexander (1818–1895)

All people that on earth do dwell[1]

1 All people that on earth do dwell,
  sing to the Lord with cheerful voice;
  him serve with fear, his praise forth tell,
  come ye before him and rejoice.

2 The Lord, ye know, is God indeed,
  without our aid he did us make;
  we are his folk, he doth us feed
  and for his sheep he doth us take.

3 O enter then his gates with praise,
  approach with joy his courts unto;
  praise, laud and bless his name always,
  for it is seemly so to do.

4 For why? The Lord our God is good:
  his mercy is for ever sure;
  his truth at all times firmly stood,
  and shall from age to age endure.

5 To Father, Son and Holy Ghost,
  the God whom heav'n and earth adore,
  from us and from the angel-host
  be praise and glory evermore.

Words by William Kethe (d. 1594)

---

[1] www.cyberhymnal.org/htm/a/1/allpeopl.htm

The wedding readings

Here's a selection of readings for you to browse through and enjoy together. You may find that one or two jump out at you as somehow resonating with who you are and your own situation. Some are from different books of the Bible and some are from other sources.

Readings from the Bible

From Genesis 1:26-28 – New Revised Standard Version (NRSV)

Then God said, 'Let us make humankind in our image, according to our likeness; and let them have dominion over the fish of the sea, and over the birds of the air, and over the cattle, and over all the wild animals of the earth, and over every creeping thing that creeps upon the earth.'

So God created humankind in his image,
in the image of God he created them;
male and female he created them.

God blessed them, and God said to them, 'Be fruitful and multiply, and fill the earth and subdue it; and have dominion over the fish of the sea and over the birds of the air and over every living thing that moves upon the earth.'

From Song of Solomon 2:10-13 – New International Version (NIV)

My lover spoke and said to me,
'Arise, my darling, my beautiful one,
and come with me.
See! The winter is past;
the rains are over and gone.
Flowers appear on the earth;
the season of singing has come,
the cooing of doves is heard in our land.
The fig-tree forms its early fruit;
the blossoming vines spread their fragrance.
Arise, come, my darling;
my beautiful one, come with me.'

From Song of Solomon 8:6-7 (NRSV)

Set me as a seal upon your heart,
as a seal upon your arm;
for love is strong as death,
passion fierce as the grave.
Its flashes are flashes of fire,
a raging flame.
Many waters cannot quench love,
neither can floods drown it.
If one offered for love all the wealth of one's house,
it would be utterly scorned.

Tobit 8:4-8 – Revised English Bible (REB)

After they were left alone and the door was shut, Tobias got up from the bed, saying to Sarah, 'Rise, my love; let us pray and beseech our Lord to show us mercy and keep us in safety.' She got up, and they began to pray that they might be kept safe. Tobias said, 'We praise you, God of our fathers, we praise your name for ever and ever. Let the heavens and all your creation praise you for ever. You made Adam and also Eve his wife, who was to be his partner and support; and those two were the parents of the human race. This was your word: "It is not good for the man to be alone; let us provide a partner suited to him." So now I take this my beloved to wife, not out of lust but in true marriage. Grant that she and I may find mercy and grow old together.'

Romans 8:35, 37-39 (NIV)

Who shall separate us from the love of Christ? Shall trouble or hardship or persecution or famine or nakedness or danger or sword?

No, in all these things we are more than conquerors through him who loved us. For I am convinced that neither death nor life, neither angels nor demons, neither the present nor the future, nor any powers, neither height nor depth, nor anything else in all creation, will be able to separate us from the love of God that is in Christ Jesus our Lord.

Romans 12:2, 9-13 (NRSV)

Do not be conformed to this world, but be transformed by the renewing of your minds, so that you may discern what is the will of God – what is good and acceptable and perfect.

Let love be genuine; hate what is evil, hold fast to what is good; love one another with mutual affection; outdo one another in showing honour. Do not lag in zeal, be ardent in spirit, serve the Lord. Rejoice in hope, be patient in suffering, persevere in prayer. Contribute to the needs of the saints; extend hospitality to strangers.

Romans 15:5-7, 13 (NRSV)

May the God of steadfastness and encouragement grant you to live in harmony with one another, in accordance with Christ Jesus, so that together you may with one voice glorify the God and Father of our Lord Jesus Christ.

Welcome one another, therefore, just as Christ has welcomed you, for the glory of God.

May the God of hope fill you with all joy and peace in believing, so that you may abound in hope by the power of the Holy Spirit.

1 Corinthians 13:1-2, 4-end (NIV)

If I speak in the tongues of men and of angels, but have not love, I am only a resounding gong or a clanging cymbal. If I have the gift of prophecy and can fathom all mysteries and all knowledge, and if I have a faith that can move mountains, but have not love, I am nothing.

Love is patient, love is kind. It does not envy, it does not boast, it is not proud. It is not rude, it is not self-seeking, it is not easily angered, it keeps no record of wrongs. Love does not delight in evil but rejoices with the truth. It always protects, always trusts, always hopes, always perseveres.

Love never fails. But where there are prophecies, they will cease; where there are tongues, they will be stilled; where there is knowledge, it will pass away. For we know in part and we prophesy in part, but when perfection comes, the imperfect disappears. When I was a child, I talked like a child, I thought like a child, I reasoned like a child. When I became a man, I put childish ways behind me. Now we see but a poor reflection as in a mirror; then we shall see face to face. Now I know in part; then I shall know fully, even as I am fully known.

And now these three remain: faith, hope and love. But the greatest of these is love.

Ephesians 3:14-end (NIV)

For this reason I kneel before the Father, from whom his whole family in heaven and on earth derives its name. I pray that out of his glorious riches he may strengthen you with power through his Spirit in your inner being, so that Christ may dwell in your hearts through faith. And I pray that you, being rooted and established in love, may have power, together with all the saints, to grasp how wide and long and high and deep is the love of Christ, and to know this love that surpasses knowledge – that you may be filled to the measure of all the fullness of God.

Now to him who is able to do immeasurably more than all we ask or imagine, according to his power that is at work within us, to him be glory in the church and in Christ Jesus throughout all generations, for ever and ever! Amen.

Philippians 4:4-8 (NRSV)

Rejoice in the Lord always; again I will say, Rejoice. Let your gentleness be known to everyone. The Lord is near. Do not worry about anything, but in everything by prayer and supplication with thanksgiving let your requests be made known to God. And the peace of God, which surpasses all understanding, will guard your hearts and your minds in Christ Jesus.

Finally, beloved, whatever is true, whatever is honourable, whatever is just, whatever is pure, whatever is pleasing, whatever is commendable, if there is any excellence and if there is anything worthy of praise, think about these things.

Colossians 3:12-17 (NRSV)

As God's chosen ones, holy and beloved, clothe yourselves with compassion, kindness, humility, meekness, and patience. Bear with one another and, if anyone has a complaint against another, forgive each other; just as the Lord has forgiven you, so you also must forgive. Above all, clothe yourselves with love, which binds everything together in perfect harmony. And let the peace of Christ rule in your hearts, to which indeed you were called in the one body. And be thankful. Let the word of Christ dwell in you richly; teach and admonish one another in all wisdom; and with gratitude in your hearts sing psalms, hymns, and spiritual songs to God. And whatever you do, in word or deed, do everything in the name of the Lord Jesus, giving thanks to God the Father through him.

1 John 4:7-12 – Authorised Version (AV)

Beloved, let us love one another: for love is of God; and every one that loveth is born of God, and knoweth God.

He that loveth not knoweth not God; for God is love.

In this was manifested the love of God towards us, because that God sent his only begotten Son into the world, that we might live through him.

Herein is love, not that we have loved God, but that he loved us, and sent his Son to be the propitiation for our sins. Beloved, if God so loved us, we ought also to love one another.

No man hath seen God at any time. If we love one another, God dwelleth in us, and his love is perfected in us.

Mark 10:6-9, 13-16 (NRSV)

'From the beginning of creation, "God made them male and female." "For this reason a man shall leave his father and mother and be joined to his wife, and the two shall become one flesh." So they are no longer two, but one flesh. Therefore what God has joined together, let no one separate.'

People were bringing little children to him in order that he might touch them; and the disciples spoke sternly to them. But when Jesus saw this, he was indignant and said to them, 'Let the little children come to me; do not stop them; for it is to such as these that the kingdom of God belongs. Truly I tell you, whoever does not receive the kingdom of God as a little child will never enter it.' And he took them up in his arms, laid his hands on them, and blessed them.

John 2:1-11 (NIV)

On the third day a wedding took place at Cana in Galilee. Jesus' mother was there, and Jesus and his disciples had also been invited to the wedding. When the wine was gone, Jesus' mother said to him, 'They have no more wine.'

'Dear woman, why do you involve me?' Jesus replied. 'My time has not yet come.'

His mother said to the servants, 'Do whatever he tells you.'

Nearby stood six stone water jars, the kind used by the Jews for ceremonial washing, each holding from twenty to thirty gallons.

Jesus said to the servants, 'Fill the jars with water'; so they filled them to the brim.

Then he told them, 'Now draw some out and take it to the master of the banquet.'

They did so, and the master of the banquet tasted the water that had been turned into wine. He did not realise where it had come from, though the servants who had drawn the water knew. Then he called the bridegroom aside and said, 'Everyone brings out the choice wine first and then the cheaper wine after the guests have had too much to drink; but you have saved the best till now.'

This, the first of his miraculous signs, Jesus performed in Cana of Galilee. He thus revealed his glory, and his disciples put their faith in him.

John 15:9-12 (AV)

As the Father hath loved me, so have I loved you: continue ye in my love.

If ye keep my commandments, ye shall abide in my love; even as I have kept my Father's commandments, and abide in his love.

These things have I spoken unto you, that my joy might remain in you, and that your joy might be full.

This is my commandment, that ye love one another, as I have loved you.

Psalm 121 (NRSV)

I lift up my eyes to the hills –
from where will my help come?
My help comes from the Lord,
who made heaven and earth.
He will not let your foot be moved;
he who keeps you will not slumber.

He who keeps Israel
will neither slumber nor sleep.
The Lord is your keeper;
the Lord is your shade at your right hand.
The sun shall not strike you by day,
nor the moon by night.
The Lord will keep you from all evil;
he will keep your life.
The Lord will keep
your going out and your coming in
from this time on and for evermore.

Psalm 145:8-9 (NRSV)

The Lord is gracious and merciful,
slow to anger and abounding in steadfast love.
The Lord is good to all,
and his compassion is over all that he has made.

Poems

'Aedh wishes for the Cloths of Heaven' by W. B. Yeats (1865–1939)

Had I the heavens' embroider'd cloths,
enwrought with golden and silver light,
the blue and the dim and the dark cloths
of night and light and the half light,
I would spread the cloths under your feet:
but I, being poor, have only my dreams;
I have spread my dreams under your feet;
tread softly because you tread on my dreams.

By permission of A. P. Watt Ltd
on behalf of Michael B. Yeats

'The bargain' by Sir Philip Sidney (1554–1586)

My true love hath my heart, and I have his,
by just exchange one for another given:
I hold his dear, and mine he cannot miss,
there never was a better bargain driven:
my true love hath my heart, and I have his.

His heart in me keeps him and me in one,
my heart in him his thoughts and senses guides:
he loves my heart, for once it was his own,
I cherish his because in me it bides:
my true love hath my heart, and I have his.

'To My Dear and Loving Husband' by Anne Bradstreet (1612–1672)

If ever two were one, then surely we.
If ever man were lov'd by wife, then thee;
if ever wife was happy in a man,
compare with me, ye women, if you can.
I prize thy love more than whole mines of gold,
or all the riches that the East doth hold.
My love is such that rivers cannot quench,
nor ought but love from thee, give recompence.
Thy love is such I can no way repay,
the heavens reward thee manifold, I pray.
Then while we live, in love let's so persevere,
that when we live no more, we may live ever.

'My Luve's Like a Red, Red Rose' by Robert Burns (1759–1796)

O my luve's like a red, red rose,
that's newly sprung in June;
o my luve's like the melodie
that's sweetly play'd in tune.

As fair art thou, my bonnie lass,
so deep in luve am I,
and I will luve thee still, my dear,
till a'the seas gang dry.

Till a' the seas gang dry, my dear,
and the rocks melt wi' the sun;
I will luve thee still, my dear,
while the sands o' life shall run.

'How Do I Love Thee?' by Elizabeth Barrett Browning (1806–1861)

How do I love thee? Let me count the ways.
I love thee to the depth and breadth and height
my soul can reach, when feeling out of sight
for the ends of Being and ideal Grace.
I love thee to the level of everyday's
most quiet need, by sun and candlelight.

I love thee freely, as men strive for Right;
I love thee purely, as they turn from Praise.
I love thee with a passion put to use
in my old griefs, and with my childhood's faith.

I love thee with a love I seemed to lose
with my lost saints – I love thee with the breath,
smiles, tears, of all my life! – and, if God choose,
I shall but love thee better after death.

The wedding reception

Guests at a wedding may well have travelled some distance, and everyone is wanting to spend time together celebrating, so the natural human response is to eat and drink together. This is also a time when the bride and groom can welcome and thank their guests, and the guests can give their personal greetings of love and good wishes.

The venue

So the venue needs to be comfortable and suitable for the number of people – it's just as uncomfortable to be rattling around in too large an area as to be squashed together. Venues for receptions can get booked up for years ahead on Saturdays, and that's one of the reasons people are beginning to choose alternative days of the week.

Many venues are very expensive, and there are alternatives, once you start thinking more creatively. Here are some ideas to get you started . . .

- Use a venue you don't have to pay for. Either a family home, or even the home of a friend or colleague who has the space and can be persuaded to offer it as a favour, or wedding gift. (Don't forget to invite them to the wedding, though!)

- A picnic in an open, public place. Think through the possibilities of your locality – perhaps a park, the beach or village green, a hill or river. Obviously this is going to be more practical during the summer months!

- A hall or room you can book cheaply and decorate yourselves. This might include a church hall, scout hut, local community centre, school or clubroom. Decorating the place takes on a whole different dimension if there's a group of you working on it together. Feed the workers – treat everyone to a takeaway – put on some music and have a clear idea of what you want done so there's the minimum of hanging about, and then go for it. Detailed suggestions for different styles can be found from page 85 onwards.
- The cheap version of a marquee: borrow lots of gazebos and fill the garden with them. If your garden isn't that big, borrow a garden from a friend, or hire space at a campsite.

The catering

Think about whether you like the idea of a sit-down meal for you and your guests, or whether you prefer the buffet style, where people can move around and meet one another. There are advantages and disadvantages to both. Both are possible to do cheaply and with great style.

- *Bring and share.* If you really love the idea of having a big wedding reception but can't afford to feed everyone, then this is the obvious but often dismissed solution. Not everyone will need to bring food, so you only need mention the 'bring' bit to those you know would be happy to oblige. If you like, suggest they consider this their wedding gift, or part of it. Work out how much food you'll need and then ask these people to provide a green salad for eight, say, or a pot of Mexican chilli for ten. Jacket potatoes can be cooked in advance, wrapped in foil and brought in insulated boxes. Non-cooks but willing helpers might be asked to bring cheese and biscuits or a frozen dessert.
- *Takeaway meal.* Set the tables up elegantly, with lots of drapes, flowers and candles, and provide the salads and desserts by the bring and share method. The main meal can be negotiated and

ordered (well in advance) so that it's delivered on the day hot and ready to eat. Plenty of bin bags and disposable plates make for the minimum of washing up. With this method you can choose to eat Indian, Chinese, Thai, pizza, burgers or fish and chips, or a combination of several, and the surroundings transform it to high-quality restaurant at a fraction of the cost.

- *Sur l'herbe.* On the invitation express your hope that as many as possible will join the family at the grassy venue, bringing with them their wedding-style picnic. Provide lots of tablecloths and little flower arrangements, and everyone sits on the grass, picnicking.

- *Mix 'n' match.* Provide basics, like French bread, butter, salads, fruit and cheese, and order party catering platters from a super-market. If possible, take advantage of home deliveries so things are delivered straight to the venue and you cut down on the complicated logistics of transporting food.

- *Cheese and wine, or ploughman's lunch.* Keep the menu classic and simple, with lots of it and attractive surroundings.

- *All-day breakfast.* Provide milk and cereals, fruit, croissants, toast and marmalade or honey, and boiled eggs. If you borrow a catering toaster, people from the different tables can come up and replenish their own tables. Tea and coffee pots on the tables and an urn set up means that drinks can be replenished by each table as well.

- *Cream tea.* Borrow or buy tablecloths, borrow tea pots and provide scones, clotted cream, butter or spread, pots of jam, milk and sugar, and a bowl of tea bags for each table. Set the tables as in a tea shop, and print a card for each table asking one person to collect the hot water in their teapot. That way everyone can come straight in and sit down, and there aren't any long queues for food, just one person from each table trotting out with their different teapots.

Workforce

- If you are involved with any uniformed organisations or the Duke of Edinburgh's Award scheme, you could try incorporating your catering, serving and washing-up and clearing needs with a community project. Make sure all volunteers get plenty to eat and have a good time as well as learning whatever they are supposed to be learning, and give a generous donation to the group for their funds.

- Organise as much as possible to be self-service or group service.

- A group of friends may be willing to take on the washing-up or serving as part of their wedding gift, or on a rota basis through the party. Turn even the jobs into a celebration.

- Get together with another 'heavenly weddings' couple and offer to wash up at each other's wedding receptions.

The wedding stationery

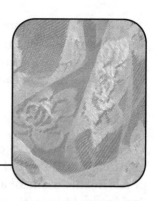

More and more this seems to be an area where people are once again enjoying getting creative. I've seen some beautiful invitations recently, computer designed or handmade. Yes, it's quite time-consuming, but it can be a very pleasant way of spending your time. Here are some ideas to get you thinking . . .

Pressed flowers and leaves

- Plan your colour scheme, toning the paper and any ribbon or lace with the colour and shape of the flowers and leaves – creams and lilac or rose, for instance, palest greens with white or cream, or magenta with grey and pink.

- It isn't only flowers that you can use. Some of the ordinary grasses look beautiful, or use tiny florets from sprays like forget-me-knots. Sometimes separate petals look like hearts, and various herbs stay sweet smelling when dried. Try rosemary sprigs or mint or lemon balm.

- Press your leaves, grasses, petals and flower heads between sheets of tissues or blotting paper, either in a purpose-built flower press or between some heavy books. Spread them out so they have plenty of space, and keep them as uncrumpled as possible as you lay them down.

- Use tweezers to pick up individual flower heads or grasses and arrange them on your card. Keep it simple and understated, rather than crammed in. Is it going straight on to the card, or will there be a fragment of paper, fabric or foil behind it? Spend a bit of time experimenting at this stage. You need to end up with a design you can put together many times over, remember!

Paper

There is a wonderful choice of paper available, including card, textured, hand-crafted paper sheets with fragments of leaf or petals inside, tissue of a whole range of colours, which can be torn and layered to create other shades, and tracing paper with a shiny or matt surface. You can also use those white, silver or gold doilies, greaseproof paper, small paper plates, wrapping paper, artwork paper, foil wrap, pieces cut from OHP acetates and brown parcel paper.

The bits and pieces

Florists' ribbon is useful as you can tear off thin lengths and coax them into curls or fold them. Try tiny pieces of lace, lining fabric, muslin or fur fabric, broderie anglaise or satin. Browse in markets for appliqué rosebuds, sequins and beads. Look at silver string, flecked wool and braid. You don't need much of anything.

Assembling

Once you've decided on the design, prepare all the ingredients and store them in different piles so you can have the assembly as an ongoing activity, doing a couple whenever you have a few minutes to spare. You can either get all the invitations to one stage before going on to the next or complete each one as you go. I reckon that's more to do with what you find most satisfying, as we all work in different ways. Don't forget to treat yourselves when you get them all completed!

Choosing a style which suits you

Once you are freed from the media pressure to conform and the rather narrow expectation of what makes for a heavenly wedding, you can think over together what style of wedding would really be right for you. And you may find you're surprised by the possibilities, all within the framework of a church wedding.

To start your imagination going, I've grouped some of the possibilities and told some stories, so you can try these weddings for size and take from the ideas whatever you like. Adapt them, change them completely, use them as a starting point. And send me a postcard from your honeymoon!

Small and special

For some people the prospect of a large wedding is so horrific that they'd rather not go for marriage at all. Some of us are by nature quite private people and find it difficult to cope with large crowds in any context, especially one which is important to us emotionally.

Sometimes it's emotional scar tissue which causes the problem. If either of you has come from a bad experience of marriage, whether your parents' or your own, you may feel a large wedding with all the trimmings may be too painful and better avoided.

Well, you can breathe a deep sigh of relief – you can still have a beautiful wedding without any of the stress of large numbers or everything being so different from usual that you feel uncomfortable and ill at ease.

Many people don't realise that they can still opt for a wedding in church, however small and simple they want it to be. But church weddings can come in all kinds of shapes and sizes – the puffy white dress isn't compulsory! Churches will be happy to accommodate you with sensitivity to both your hopes and fears.

Don't forget – the smallest possible number for a church marriage ceremony is only five people:

> the bride and bridegroom,
> the minister,
> two witnesses.

Quiet and timeless

Many churches have small beautiful side chapels where a quiet wedding can take place, so you won't be standing in the middle of a huge space and there will be no long aisle to brave. Often these chapels are the places where daily prayer has been going on for generations, so they have a very special atmosphere.

You won't need to worry about being heard or sound systems. You don't need to have any hymns or organ music, and there can be something about the very stillness and silence which manages to hold and celebrate the solemnity and joy of your wedding in a way that is timeless and focused.

If you feel that getting married like this is really in tune with your style . . .

Consider getting married

- on a weekday
- in the early morning – from 8am – followed by a wedding breakfast
- in the early evening – up to 6pm – followed by a wedding supper

Consider wearing
- clothes you feel comfortable in
- clothes you choose together
- clothes you will wear often
- a simple dress made by yourself or a friend

Consider inviting
- only two witnesses
- only immediate family and friends
- a friend to take a few pictures

And if you want some music
- use recorded chamber music
- consider harp, harpsichord or classical guitar

And if you want flowers
- carry a small bunch of your favourite flowers, tied with a length of muslin, or a single lily or rose
- buy flowers from a supermarket and arrange them in small containers
- rather than flowers, go for candlelight, with clusters of candles on window sills and behind the altar or holy table (candles standing on mirrors double the effect)

And for transport consider
- walking to the church, either separately with friends and family or together
- asking a friend or family member to drive you
- taking a taxi and paying up front (order in advance to be sure)
- using public transport

Follow the wedding with

- a romantic meal somewhere beautiful
- a day's walking in the hills and pub lunch
- a day's sailing or a boat trip
- an hour's private plane flight
- a balloon ride
- a visit to somewhere beautiful
- tea and wedding cake with the family

The special in the ordinary

An unusual possibility for those who really dread the 'big fuss' ceremony is for your wedding or wedding blessing to happen in a relaxed way during an ordinary church service, either Sunday morning or evening, or during a quiet midweek service.

You've probably never even considered this as an option, as it's hardly ever done now, but that's no reason for it not happening if it suits you best. After all, many christenings (baptisms) now take place in the context of a Sunday service.

The advantages of a wedding like this is that there is a lovely sense of doing something special in the context of ordinary weekly worship – and isn't that what marriage is all about – the special in the ordinary? The actual marriage ceremony isn't long, and can be easily fitted into the service either about halfway through, like a christening, or, if you're going to be very nervous and would find it easier to cope with, near the beginning, so you can relax and enjoy the rest of the service.

Sunday services vary in style from church to church, but churches are generally friendly places, willing to welcome a bride and groom among them. And if you are wanting to get married or have your marriage blessed at the church you normally attend, this will be an important celebration in the life of the whole church community.

You won't need to make a grand entrance down the aisle (unless you want to). You can be sitting in the pews until it's time to come and stand together for the vows.

And afterwards, if you are only a small group, and aren't planning a wedding party somewhere else, most churches have refreshments after a service, so a piece of wedding cake offered with the coffee, or a glass of mulled wine, if it isn't an alcohol-free church, will allow you to celebrate with very little preparation or expense, but oceans of support and goodwill. As soon as you want to you can take your leave and all the happy memories with you.

Using special days

Many Anglican, Roman Catholic and Methodist churches have a quiet service of Morning or Evening Prayer nearly every day, and a service of Holy Communion during the week, and you may like to consider getting married during one of these services, on a particular date or festival which has special significance for you. Provided the wedding takes place between the legally stipulated hours of 8am and 6pm there should be no problem. Bear in mind that the priest or minister must have a rest day which isn't a Sunday, and there are many other pastoral commitments to fit into the week, so be flexible – you may not necessarily be able to have your first choice of date.

There was a time when weddings on Christmas Day or Epiphany (Twelfth Night) became very popular, and this was partly possible because they were much simpler affairs than we have become used to. Go back to the simple and you might once again be able to entertain the possibility of a Christmas morning family wedding, with the carols and candlelight of a festive Christmas Day service, followed by a family Christmas dinner.

Big community weddings

Checking out the average prices for a professionally done large wedding may have left you feeling trapped: it looks as if you're going to have to cut down drastically on the numbers and leave out lots of those you really wanted to be included. That's pretty depressing.

Not necessarily. Use the principles and ideas for doing things in-house and the large wedding you wanted again becomes possible. Here are some examples to encourage you.

April 'Global' wedding with 200 guests

Style: classic
Colours: cream and lilac

The bride had four bridesmaids. Fabric for the dresses was bought in Newham and the dresses made mainly by the bride and bridesmaids themselves to a simple classic pattern – long straight skirts and separate tops. The bride wore cream silk covered by fine embroidered muslin. All four bridesmaids wore matching cream silk skirts, with a lilac sheen. The two blonde bridesmaids had lilac silk tops and the dark haired ones cream silk tops. A tiara for the bride and the wedding rings had been bought while on holiday in Bangladesh. Matching shoes were made to measure and colour in Vietnam, bought while visiting there.

The bride carried white lilies, creamy pink rosebuds, sprays of lilac and gypsophila. Each of the bridesmaids carried a posy of creamy pink rosebuds, lilac and gypsophila. Flowers were done by the bride's mother.

The bridegroom had two best men – his brothers. In Vietnam suits were made for the groom, best men, groom's father and brother-in-law, with lilac and cream waistcoats. Lilac cravats were bought locally.

Invitations were handmade by the bride and groom, using paper bought in Vietnam and flowers pressed from the garden and a local florist. The wording was produced on Microsoft Word™. Service sheets were done at home on computer and copied locally, folded and stapled by visiting friends.

As the church was full of Easter flowers there was no need for extra flowers, and the church flower arranger kindly included some lilac in her arrangements. Lilac and greenery was provided from neighbours' gardens.

The church was packed with family and friends and took place in the context of a Communion service, which both bride and bridegroom wanted. The bridegroom was driven in his family's car, and the bride and bridesmaids gathered at the bride's family home and walked the short distance to the church.

Tabletop flower arrangements were made by a group of friends and family, with everyone watching a demonstration as a model. Set in small foil dishes the flowers and foliage were partly from the garden and partly from the florist and supermarket. Extra arrangements were made for the washbasins in the church hall.

The bride's hen night was a day at a health and leisure centre, making use of a special offer from the Boots™ points scheme. The groom's stag night was a visit to the local casino. Unusually, everyone then joined up for a meal at a noodle bar, before working together on the decoration of the hall, transforming it in a couple of hours.

A rope strung up along the centre of the hall meant that rolls of paper tablecloths could be draped over at regular intervals, transforming the hall into a marquee. Ivy, small flower arrangements and lilac candles were spread along the windowsills. Trestle tables covered with cream cloths and lilac over-cloths were laid with cutlery borrowed from the church hall and paper plates. Tabletop flower arrangements and more lilac and cream candles and balloons made the hall into an exclusive restaurant setting. Quantities of lilac net were gathered and entwined around the stair rails.

Toilets were cleaned and washbasins decorated with flowers – tiny posies in plastic milk bottle lids – and lilac handwash, soap and handcream provided along with cream towels, borrowed for the occasion.

A friend had been asked to take photographs and she had been given a list of the groupings the bride and groom wanted included. Everyone helped gather the people for each group picture.

Wine (bought whenever there was a discount at the local super-market) and wedding cake (made by a colleague) were available straight after the service, and after a while the guests were greeted as they made their way into the decorated hall. The starter, salads and desserts had been brought by guests, and fish and chips ordered from the local chippy. Some of the teenagers gave a gift of collecting the disposable things and washing up the rest.

Money saved from this in-house, community approach enabled them to book a harpist for the service, playing as the bride and bridesmaids walked up the aisle, during the signing of the registers, and as the bridal party processed outside. The simple, gentle elegance of this fitted beautifully with the character and style of the wedding party. They were also able to book a band for the evening, and after the meal everyone helped clear the tables to the side for dancing.

The result of some careful forward planning and creative thinking was a lavish and very gracious, elegant wedding, owned and enjoyed by everybody there. And the cost was kept low.

July 'Pastoral' wedding with 200 guests

Style: Fresh and natural
Colour: Meadow flowers

The bride and groom belonged to the church community and very much wanted everyone to share in their celebration. But there wasn't much money available, only plenty of goodwill.

The bride had one bridesmaid – her sister. Being involved in children's clubs meant that there were too many children to choose as bridesmaids and pages without leaving some out. So, instead, shiny gift bags were given to all the children invited, with sweets and a pot of bubble mix in, and a letter asking them to enjoy the sweets and fill the bag with flower petals to bring to the wedding with the bubbles. As the wedding party walked out of the church, the children crowded around scattering their petals and blowing their bubbles all over the bride and bridegroom.

The bride's dress was white satin, fitted and flared with a train, and tiny pearl buttons all down the back. This would have been a very expensive item, except that it was made for her by her sister. On her head she wore a circlet of pink rosebuds, cornflowers, sage, rosemary and Marguerite daisies. She carried a sheaf of flowers, some from the florist, some from the garden, with pink roses, cornflowers, daisies, gypsophila, sage, lavender, mint and rosemary. Her bridesmaid wore a fitted, creamy gold dress. She wore flowers in her hair and carried a posy of flowers and herbs. The bride's mother did the flowers.

The bridegroom and best man wore dark suits with white shirt and silk tie, and a spray of rose, rosemary and cornflower.

Wedding rings for bride and groom had been bought in a sale from Past Times for £35 each.

Single-use cameras were distributed for guests to take photographs, and a family friend made a sound recording of the service. During the signing of the registers there was some beautiful singing: a solo from a gifted 14-year-old friend and two songs the children had been specially practising.

The church hall had been set out with small tables covered with bright tablecloths, borrowed from the community of guests, and laid with borrowed tea sets for a cream tea. This had to be done on the day of the wedding, once the church hall ballet classes had finished, so a working party of friends and family – including the bride still in jeans – took this on at top speed right up to an hour before the service! One family of friends had taken on the decorating of the church and hall as their wedding gift, which included pew-end flowers, and paper sunflowers up the hall stairs. Family members made the little flower arrangements for the tables.

Later there was a barn dance, with a buffet meal – a mixture of salads, cheeses, cold meats and jacket potatoes with bowls of pick-your-own strawberries and raspberries. Family and friends shared the catering and the clearing up afterwards. As much as possible was disposable to ease the washing-up. During the evening the bridal couple were driven down to the local station where they left for their honeymoon by train – to a very old cottage at Whitby, where the owner had left a bottle of champagne.

This was very much a sunny, 'all-ages' wedding, with games as well as dancing, and everyone involved, even in the service. And the cost? Not much over £1000.

Something slightly different . . .

Maybe you feel you'd like to break out of the usual and do things a little differently. Well, here are a few ideas to get you thinking!

A wedding in the context of a journey

Gather with all the guests at a point some distance from the church and walk with a few jazz or classical musicians (or recorded music) in a full bridal procession. Encourage everyone to bring large umbrellas in case of rain. After the service a hired coach takes everyone to a picnic and partying venue.

A wedding with a theme

The theme is reflected in everything from the invitations to the send-off, and may be as simple as a colour range, or more specific, such as . . .

Seaside

- Make invitations using a little sand and tiny shells stuck on to blue card, or torn layers of blue and green tissue paper on shiny silver card.

- Give children a copiable sheet to make themselves a wedding windmill.
- Child bridesmaids and pages carry small beach buckets filled with flowers.
- An arrangement of shells, stones and sand on a mirror, with small potted plants and grasses around it among the stones. Put down heavy-duty plastic sheet under the whole thing.
- As people are coming in, have the sound of the sea playing and a projected image of the sea.
- Order sticks of rock for everyone, with the names of bride and groom going all the way through.
- Have a beach party reception.

Country meadow
- Arrangements of daisies, roses, cornflowers and buttercups in the church.
- Coronet for the bride and buttonhole for the groom of daisies and buttercups, freshly picked.
- Play recorded birdsong as people are coming in to the church.
- If there is a screen, projected images of meadow flowers, either using PowerPoint™ or a printed acetate and overhead projector.
- Reception on a village green, in a country park or in a garden.

Rainforest
- Make invitations by cutting out a string of leaf shapes which unfold from a tissue paper flower.
- Ask people to bring flower petals as confetti.
- Arrangements of greenery and large bright flowers, with painted wooden parrots among the flowers.

- The bride wears orchid or hibiscus in her hair, and carries a looped 'creeper' of greenery and hibiscus blooms. The bridegroom wears a hibiscus in a buttonhole.
- Make a bridal train which falls from the neck like a waterfall.
- Play recorded sounds of a rainforest as people come in – natural sound CDs often combine sounds and appropriate music.
- Project images of sun shining through the canopy of a rainforest and close-ups of flowers, trees and birds.
- Visit a rainforest on your honeymoon – there's always the Eden Project in Cornwall or the gardens in Edinburgh if you don't want to travel too far.

Tropical island

- Come in to Hawaiian music played over the sound of the ocean.
- If there's a screen or suitable blank wall, project an image of palm trees, beach and ocean.
- Have the parents presenting the bride and groom with necklace chains of fresh flowers after the signing of the register.
- Bridegroom wears a white suit or Indian sherwani, the bride a long white sarong with bare feet and an anklet. Flowers in her hair.
- Include fresh coconut, pineapple and mango in the food – and in the flower arrangement in church.
- Place tropical fragranced liquid soap and handcream in the bathroom.
- Visit a jacuzzi as part of the hen night.

A period of history – for example, Victorian, Regency, 1960s
- Design an invitation which sets the scene. Lace and ribbon, elegant pastel stripes, psychedelic or whatever.
- Invite guests to 'dress the age', at least in a token way – interesting waistcoat, tie, coloured or lace handkerchief, shawl, flowers or long dress, for instance.

A hobby shared by the bride and groom
- Dance down the aisle.
- Travel by bicycle.
- *Match of the Day* as music to walk out of the church.
- Birdsong as you walk into the church.
- Sail away.
- Grow the bouquet.

Cutting the cost of wedding stress

Hopes and fears

Weddings can be stressful in the extreme. The fact that you have chosen to marry each other means that you are pretty passionate about wanting to spend the rest of your lives together in a happy marriage. Precisely because the starting point of your marriage – your wedding day – is so special and important and life-changing, your aim is for it to be perfect in every way.

Once that is the established goal, there grows an accompanying fear that it might be ruined by things going wrong – even that things going wrong on the wedding day may in some shadowy and frightening way affect the outcome of the marriage itself.

Fear and superstition go hand in hand with dreams and longings, and we need to be aware of that darker side of our deepest hopes, so that when we discover some of these rather sinister, unexplained anxieties popping up to the surface as the wedding preparations gather pace, we may recognise them for what they are and face them confidently. They are a normal, natural side effect to wanting a good thing with all our heart.

So don't let the fears take hold. Count them as a mark of how much you genuinely long for a good and lasting marriage with the person you love, and be comforted by the truth that actually the wedding is only part of the first day of your long and happy marriage. Yes, it will be lovely for things to go well at that time of celebration and commitment, but it isn't a perfect wedding that will make a marriage good. Enjoy it to the full, but don't make it carry more than it's designed for.

Heavy investment

Another stress factor is the extent to which you and your family are investing hard cash in this day of days. Financial investment inevitably raises the expectation of a good return for your money, and in wedding terms that can easily translate into such (often unvoiced) fear and resentment as . . .

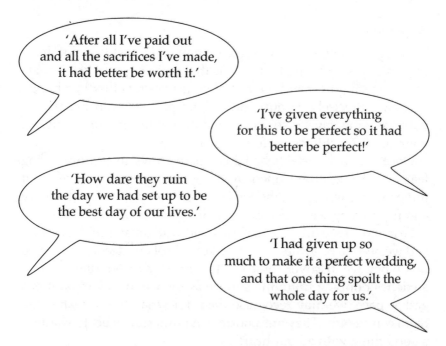

I am really concerned about the widespread way that unrealistic expectations and assumptions set people up for disappointment. Money can't buy a perfect day, and a perfect day is not actually about everything going exactly according to plan using the most expensive options. In fact, it's often the opposite. If we set out with a less inflated expectation of fairyland perfection, and allow ourselves to be more interested in investing in the marriage than the wedding day, we are far less likely to be thrown by things turning out differently from what we expected at the wedding, and we'll enjoy the day more.

Of course, it's perfectly possible to spend a fortune *and* have a wonderful wedding, but, in my experience over the years, there is often extra tension and disappointment where *expensive* and *perfect* have been mistakenly assumed to be synonymous.

The battle of the dreams

As soon as the intention to marry is mentioned, emotions and dreams are activated in people. Lots of these dreams are highly charged and dearly cherished. Any wedding-related emotional scar tissue can start aching, and old emotional wounds can suddenly open up again. Everyone has their own ideas about what must or must not happen at a wedding for it to carry such a special and important celebration.

The difficulty for you, as the bridal couple, is fielding all these well-meant and understandable pressures to have the wedding of everyone else's dream, rather than yours. The first important thing to know is this:

You can't please everyone!

No matter how hard you try, how many sacrifices or compromises you make, it is impossible to please everyone, and if you realise that early on in the planning it will save you some stress. You'll be a little more relaxed about it when the points of difference and tension inevitably start showing. It is, after all, *your* marriage, and so it's very important that the wedding reflects what *you* feel about it, even if that isn't the prescribed and assumed recipe that everyone else wants for you because it was right for them.

In the early days, listen to all the suggestions but don't commit yourselves. The 'Yes, we'll think about that – we're not deciding anything just yet' line is useful and doesn't set up expectations that a suggestion has been taken up.

Be kind but firm. Remind people affectionately that you appreciate them wanting the best for you. Enlist their help by asking them to do something for you at the wedding.

Keeping communication channels open

Lots of upsets and misunderstandings can happen among friends and family through not communicating enough. And that's especially true at a time of something special and important like a wedding. It's easy to see how it happens. We're chatting to all kinds of people about the wedding arrangements and often think we've already told one set of people when it was someone else we were talking to. Suddenly someone feels excluded.

We all feel safe and loved if we're included and upset if we sense we've been excluded, and keeping everyone informed is one of the best ways of keeping them happy.

Also, communicating regularly prevents a build-up of any anxieties or misunderstandings. It clears the air as you go along and reinforces the shared ownership of the day.

A regular emailed or web-page update can be useful for some, and popping round for a chat and a drink works for others. Ask a few people from different 'sides' of the family to look at the words you're using in the invitations and service sheet, just in case you've inadvertently included or left out something which might cause problems.

Look at things like the form of your names, the order, whose son or daughter the invitation refers to – are those who need to be mentioned all included? Do some invitations need to be sent out with a covering letter – that although you understand they may well not be able to come in person, you wanted them to share in everything as far as possible, including the invitation.

Is the circle of relatives from each family fairly worked out – it will help to keep the same boundaries for both extended families, so as to avoid upsetting third cousins twice removed. You may want to make it clear to the wider circle of your family and friends, whom you can't fit in to the reception, that you'd love to see them at the wedding service itself.

Give everyone plenty of time when you ask them to do anything or be involved in some way. Although some of us thrive on the excitement and flexibility of 'spur of the moment' ideas, many find it desperately stressful to have something thrown at them at the last minute but take enormous pleasure in planning slowly and carefully and having it sorted ages in advance. It isn't that either approach is right or wrong, they're just different. And it's a good job we're all different – life would be pretty boring if we weren't.

So recognise the different way people work, respect the validity of all, and as far as possible involve people in ways they'll enjoy and feel confident with. Encourage the others and be encouraged by them yourselves. And laugh. Sometimes that's the best way of defusing explosive situations. It is only a wedding, after all.

Dealing with family feuds

Hopefully you belong to a family where everyone is still talking to each other. However, the reality is that in most families it isn't all plain sailing and there are often those who find it difficult to get on together. If either set of parents are separated or divorced there are likely to be some areas which will take gracious and sensitive handling.

Do bear in mind that if those who love you both are already feeling hurt by another situation, they may overreact or be more upset than you might expect from any number of wedding-related incidences. That's human nature – a natural reaction to being hurt is to become defensive and touchy. Look beyond the prickles.

If there's an overreaction which comes out as anger or criticism against you or your partner, it's naturally going to affect you and set up a counter-reaction. You'll probably feel hurt and upset and angry yourself and spring into defensive action mode, ready to retaliate as nastily as possible! Like I said, that's normal human nature.

But if you want things to get better, not worse, there are ways to bring that about. Make yourself calm, breathe deeply and physically relax your face and shoulder muscles. Give yourself space. You probably know why this person is feeling insecure or hurt, so remember where they're coming from and make allowances, responding to what's really going on, rather than this half-related undeserved outburst. It may, for instance, be reassurance they need, rather than counter-attack!

Don't forget that both you and they are valid as people and that it's more productive in the long run to respect one another, even if that means agreeing to differ. Talking things out calmly and honestly is enormously healing for everyone. The aim is that all involved are winners, with no one feeling either triumphant or crushed.

In extreme family circumstances consider having a small 'thanksgiving for marriage' service at a later date for the part of the family living in another area of the world.

Overwork

You are going to need plenty of sleep and time to relax and unwind, so book it in. Especially if both of you are working full-time, commuting and with full lives, you may find the months of wedding preparation start getting to you both and coming out as irritation and arguments.

See if there's any activity or responsibility which it might be sensible to put down for a while as the wedding approaches, so as to give you a bit more time and space.

Keep a box file for everything to do with the wedding so you don't lose important documents or ideas and have to waste frustrating time searching through your clumps of in-tray around the house.

Spread the load of what needs doing and make up a kind of simple spreadsheet to schedule things. It will save you worrying about trying to keep everything in your head.

Don't take on more than you can do together. Counting the cost of a wedding needs to include counting the cost of time and energy as well as money. It may be that for you both to stay sane and happy it's better to go for something more simple (not necessarily smaller and certainly not less heavenly!) rather than the wedding becoming an exhausting occasion. Weddings are not meant to be exhausting and draining. They're meant to be uplifting and happy celebrations. Don't let them get out of hand and rule you. You and your marriage are what really matter.

Getting to know you

It may well be that the families of bride and bridegroom don't know each other very well. A marriage does bring both families into a new relationship, and the wedding preparation time is a good opportunity to start getting to know one another better.

Sometimes everyone hits it off brilliantly straightaway, and I know several families who have become close personal friends as a result of their son and daughter getting married. When that happens it's an extra wedding present and something to be very thankful for. It certainly is a great blessing as the new family grows, and the 'in-laws' are rightly named and supportive, rather than becoming negative 'out-laws'.

But, of course, there's no guarantee that simply because you and your beloved adore one another, your families will automatically become close as well. The tensions can be highlighted because you are so much wanting there to be a good extended family relationship, and at the same time you may have had a sneaking suspicion that the sparks may fly, that there may be jealousies and competition for affection, and all those other human things that disrupt harmonious living.

So how can we ease these kinds of tensions and cut the stress cost?

I recommend that you start by diagnosing the hardening of the 'oughteries'. There is no 'ought' about your families feeling attracted to each other. Sometimes it happens and sometimes it doesn't. So keep the hopes shining but notch down the assumptions. The more relaxed atmosphere will help friendships grow.

Don't force the pace. It's important that both families meet, and cards, emails and phone calls from time to time are polite as well as friendly. I'm all for being polite – it's the way we act out our respect for another person, whether they're strangers or those we live with.

If there's a common interest – apart from the obvious – perhaps you could arrange to meet up in connection with that. Have a drink or a meal together. Meet up at somewhere relaxing and comfortable for everyone. Share some of the family photo albums, and get to know a little more of the life which led everyone to this point.

As trust builds, relationships flourish. It's the lack of trust and any sense of being threatened that makes for hostility and barriers. Work at building bridges instead of walls.

The conflict monster

For many of us, the prospect of any kind of conflict is unnerving. It's the very last thing we want and we try to avoid it at all costs. Conflict is often perceived by all kinds of people, male and female, as a monster – destructive and damaging, threatening our survival or the survival of a precious relationship.

The downside of this perception is that sometimes it can lead to healthy conflict being shut away and squashed into the cellar. We might tell ourselves we're avoiding it, but usually we're just burying it somewhere deep inside, and unless it's dealt with properly, it can suddenly fly out and hit us when we're not prepared and shock us with its intensity.

What do I mean by healthy conflict? Well, the normal and healthy way for humans to live is in a social context. We survive by looking out for one another's needs, responding to one another and working together. An important part of that is learning to understand one another, and we do that by discovering what the others like and dislike. We discover about the real nature of freedom – there are boundaries where my freedom curtails another's. Maturity is learning to respect one another's boundaries. Conflicts are built into this process, just as falling off a bicycle one side or the other is built into the way we learn about balance.

Often our fear of conflict has its roots somewhere back in our learning process, where perhaps we were prevented either from recognising our own valid space or that of others. If the learning process was ever perceived as being too dangerous, we took the safer option and pretended. Or we learnt that from observing the behaviour of someone close to us.

So the truth about conflict is that it's rather like fire. Out of hand it is indeed dangerous and potentially deadly, but when used properly it gives light in darkness, and warms where there is coldness.

Much in the stressful situations we've been looking at involves facing a problem candidly, and calmly voicing how we're perceiving things, our concerns, fears and anxieties, the reasons for our irritation and feelings of anger or humiliation.

Alongside this is calmly listening to the other person, trying to hear where the gaps in communication or perception are, and working towards a better understanding of one another. That may mean the outcome involves both of you in the generosity of some kind of compromise. It may bring a voiced recognition of where there has been an innocent mistake or a lack of thoughtfulness. It will certainly involve forgiveness – and a willingness to move forward instead of getting stuck in the hurting place.

Life is just too short to spend it jammed into the dead end of unresolved conflicts. Get them sorted as you go along and you'll be able to travel lightly and freely, with the conflict monster a pet poodle.

Preparing yourselves for your marriage

How well do you know each other? As part of your wedding preparations, it's not a bad idea to check that you've talked through together some of the things which may become important to you during your marriage.

Not that either of you is likely to stay with exactly the same attitudes and opinions through to old age, of course – how grim would that be! But it does help your marriage off to a good start if there aren't any crucial points of violent, unresolved disagreement between you as you make your vows of lasting commitment.

The other point perhaps worth making is that sometimes couples approach marriage assuming that they will be able to change things in their partner's behaviour or personality. Disillusion starts creeping in as it becomes increasingly obvious that the changing is never going to happen. Far better to marry because you love and accept the other person just as they are, knowing what they are like. And far better to postpone or call off the marriage if either of you has changed your mind. Yes, that's horribly painful, but far less painful than going through with something you know in your heart of hearts is wrong for you.

It's likely that you will have talked over most things to your satisfaction already, and that's partly what has made you decide on this step of marriage. You both feel comfortable enough with one another to travel the years together.

What does your partner think about having children, for instance? What do you think yourself? What are your hopes and horrors about having a family?

There's a whole lot of issues connected with becoming parents, many of which you really won't know how you feel about until faced with particular situations. But at least get in touch with your gut feelings and talk through some of the things which you both need to share. It's quite possible for one partner to assume that the other shares a dream of a huge family, closely spaced, while in fact they're horrified at the prospect of countless babies and toddlers cluttering up the home, and 'wanting children' means in their own dream two kids, widely spaced out in years.

And what if the children don't come easily? Is adoption or fostering a dream – or even a calling – or is one of you worried that you'd find it hard to accept that as an option. What about IVF?

If either of you has children already, there are important things to talk over honestly. This is not the time for pretending. Share both the joys and the difficult patches, so that you can move forward into the new future without any unaired ghosts.

Some couples have found it really valuable to do a personality profile indicator course – such as Myers-Briggs – together, as it helps them understand and appreciate the different ways each approaches life. That in turn makes it easier to use one another's strengths in the marriage and not be thrown by the things which inevitably jar. It also enables you to laugh at yourselves and see the funny side of those preferred ways of doing things.

We're all a mix of nurture as well as nature, and it's good to recognise in ourselves and in each other the things that have shaped us, made us strong in some areas and vulnerable in others. Our past affects who we are in the present and how we will deal with the future.

As you approach marriage, you are preparing to commit yourselves to a close family relationship with another human being who probably hasn't known you all your life. That may be a distinct advantage! We often go through stages that we might prefer to forget or wish we'd done differently. But you do need to know about one another's past, especially the kind of experiences that you know have influenced you or affected you deeply.

Part of the trust between you both is feeling able when necessary to talk about the difficult and disturbing things without fear. So what about your past? How sensible is it to pretend or edit that? Be honest with each other now and you'll be building strong foundations. Lie at this stage and you'll be building on sand.

What I'm concerned about is that you can feel at peace with one another, the kind of peace that only comes from being honest and not living in fear that some hidden bit of your past might come to light some day and ruin everything. The best way to avoid that and defuse any unexploded secrets is to trust one another now and tell out the truth.

Talk together about your hopes and dreams as well. About your beliefs and your doubts. About your ambitions and goals in life. None of this is set in stone, is it? You'll be talking together, perhaps with a shared dream taking shape as you go. It's one of the loveliest privileges of an intimate relationship that you can enjoy both the shared memories you are building, and the shared dreams for the future.

Then there are issues like spending priorities, both in time and money. How are you planning to organise your finances? Separate or joint accounts? What does 'all my worldly goods with you I share' mean for you both? If there are real, major differences of expectation, air them now and come to a proper understanding, rather than risk building resentment for later.

What about your respective cleaning habits? Does one of you feel relaxed in a super-tidy environment and the other in a tip? Arguments built on resentment about job expectations around the home are a very common cause of misery, but they don't have to be. Being honest about what you both find unbearable will help you work through to a structure which both of you can cope with. Don't forget that both your opinions are valid, and compromise is not about losing but about a shared win.

Don't let the little niggles fester away underneath. Sometimes we nobly do the loving martyr act at first, but eventually we get fed up with being martyrs, and all the accumulated resentment can suddenly burst out in a rush. Much better to deal with things as they happen, not accusingly or heavily, but simply letting one another know. It's an altogether gentler and lighter and more loving way of relating.

Talking of love and tenderness, don't forget how important it is to express your love for one another. We all need to be told we're loved and enjoyed and appreciated, and that's an ongoing need, not something we can be told once and that's enough. Making love is a whole-body way of saying, 'I love you', and that includes the way you look at each other, and touch, and listen and speak.

Be sensitive and tender with one another, gentle, spacious and passionate. There's a whole lot written about technique in love-making, but the best guide to expressing your love physically starts in the heart and between the ears. Whatever the technique, the greatest turn-off is selfishness. The greatest turn-on is mutual trust and love, so that you free one another to enjoy and play and satisfy. When we make love with the person we love, we are at our most wonderfully human, both giving and receiving at once, with both shared and individual fulfilment. The two becoming one flesh focuses our utmost longing and blissful satisfaction.

If you are intending to save a full physical expression of your love until you are married, one of the little-publicised advantages is that you become expert in those more subtle ways of love-making – the looking into one another's eyes, the touching of hands, the hugs, the kissing, the highly charged 'being together' – all of which develop a sensitivity which will greatly add to your love-making once you are married.

For many, the engagement, or moment of decision to marry, is the point at which a publicly acknowledged, full physical relationship feels most appropriate. Whatever the birth-control method used, pregnancy is still a possibility, and so it makes sense to have sex only with someone you would be happy to parent a child with. The consequences are so far-reaching that you really need to talk about this together when you're calm and rational, rather than in the heat of the moment. You don't have to drift into one particular way of living – it's your choice, and a very important choice.

Just because it's so unusual to stay celibate till marriage doesn't necessarily mean that it's unwise. In fact, surprisingly, there isn't any evidence to show that marriages work better if the couple live together first, even though it seems initially sensible to do so. The Christian teaching is that a sexual relationship is special to the marriage relationship, and the life commitment of marriage is the most stable and secure environment for it.

However, there's obviously a big difference between a couple preparing for marriage and other, casual relationships. Certainly you need to have spent time together in all kinds of situations as you prepare for marriage, including going away on holiday, sharing a kitchen and so on. This doesn't have to mean setting up home together, and, once again, you have a choice.

If you are deciding to go against the flow and wait till marriage before living together, long engagements aren't helpful. If your relationship has moved on to the marriage stage, marriage is where you need to be. You'll also need family and friendship support to stay celibate, as there is such strong pressure against this unusual arrangement. And it can be a great emotional strain trying not to express your love unreservedly for any length of time. There are financial implications, too. It may be too expensive to rent two places when you're saving hard to buy somewhere together. Timing the wedding with house-buying may be difficult.

On the other hand, there are advantages. Increasingly people are moving back home after studying away at college or university because it's cheaper. If either or both of you live in the family home you can save faster for your own place. Or if one of you is renting your new home, both of you can work on it and prepare the nest for when you both move in together after the wedding.

But the main reason for choosing to stay apart until you're married is what such a courageous choice says about your commitment to the idea of a completely new stage in your life together. There is something extraordinarily holy about it. The self-discipline and generosity needed to fly in the face of convention and keep yourselves for this holy estate of matrimony is like a fragile and beautiful gift, one to the other.

This makes it a completely different situation from when celibacy till marriage was the normal, expected route. We've gone far enough away from that to look at it as something new. Now that it isn't generally acceptable, to choose it is something particularly remarkable. Couples who have gone for it talk about their love deepening through it and the wedding itself taking on a romantic beauty and reverence which is hard to beat.

As you talk these things over together, remember that respect for one another, which will be so valuable all through your marriage. You may well disagree about these important things, but that doesn't mean you don't love one another. Sometimes you will grow to understand where your partner is coming from and sometimes you won't. But that doesn't mean you don't love one another. Part of love is accepting the other person for who they are. And one day in the future, perhaps when your grandchildren are about to get married, you'll be glad to see them talking things over together as they prepare for their wedding.

So what makes a successful marriage?

Your wedding day is important and special, but it only lasts one day. Its greatest significance is that it is the first day of your marriage. Perhaps one of the downsides of weddings having become such costly affairs is that more energy goes into that one day than into the marriage itself. But when you decided to take this step you didn't ask your beloved to have a wedding with you, you were asking them to marry you. There are still plenty of couples around who are living examples of a fulfilling and happy marriage, with years of love and affection, and a knock-on good effect on their whole extended family and in the community where they live and work.

This marriage is really what your wedding is about, isn't it? The daily coming home to one another's welcoming, and knowing the other will be pleased to see you; snuggling up together watching a film when it's cold outside; the birth and growing of your children, and grandchildren; the shared helpless laughter and the shared tears. It's the celebrations, surprises, excitements and disappointments of life all lived through hand in hand with the one you love – the one who loves you. It's knowing that you are loving and being loved for who you really are, so that together you can face the inevitable ups and downs of life with confidence. It's providing a secure and healthy environment where children thrive and guests feel comfortable and welcomed. And it's about history as well – you join the ever-widening branches of your family tree and will in time yourselves be part of your descendants' history.

'Have separate toothpaste tubes and share a bed'

That's what my mum reckoned would help make for a happy and fulfilling marriage, and I can see what she was getting at. The fact that we're all different means that there are bound to be various tensions about quite little things, and my mum was right – make life easier for yourselves by minimising those tensions wherever you can. Toothpaste tubes in her day could easily be such a source of irritation, with some people squeezing from the bottom up and others from the middle and leaving the top off! So to have separate tubes avoided that frustration. But it's important to share the really important things, and work at that even when it's difficult. Whatever has been going on during the day between you, make up before you sleep, if you possibly can. And that's easier – or at least more necessary – to do if you're sharing a bed.

Throughout your marriage there will be times when you'll need to make the boundaries clear where extended family and friends are concerned. Like they say, 'Good fences make good neighbours.' Your new marriage is in a way staking out a fresh plot of land to live in, and it's right that you are allowed the freedom and space to let your marriage grow naturally, without the interference of well-meaning but unhelpful intrusions. So protect that marriage space and don't let yourselves be bullied or possessed. Being married alters relationships not just between you and your partner but within both your families and friendships.

If you know you're really bad at holding your ground, and find it difficult to say things like, 'Thanks all the same but I'd rather do it my way,' or 'No, I'm sorry, we've arranged to have a bit of time on our own that day,' it's worth actually practising the 'script' aloud to give you confidence. Get together with a friend and practise with one being a pain, making you feel guilty, and you telling them firmly but politely whatever you really want the outcome to be. Equally, you may be one of those who needs to practise saying, 'I was wrong' out loud on your own until it loses some of its horror for you.

Some marriages that become happy and fulfilling have gone through such rocky patches that it seemed at the time they were bound to fail. Yet actually by working through those problems with the help of friends and marriage counselling, the couple are drawn closer than ever before, understanding themselves and each other far better, so that the marriage has been a source of healing for them. That's quite an encouragement – if things seem to be falling apart, don't assume it's the end of your marriage. Marriages can be carefully repaired so that they end up stronger than when they were new.

Successful marriages seem to thrive on enjoying yourselves and making some time to relax and 'play'. Families who play together stay together. Book in family time as you would any other important activity – don't slip into assuming that happens automatically just because you're under the same roof. It's quite frightening how easy it is for you to suddenly find you're spending less time with your closest loved ones than with everyone else – and that can be when things start going wrong. So make time for your relationship to stay fresh and grow. Don't stop having fun together. If you're both getting overstressed at work, cut down the hours or consider a change of job – your marriage is worth it. Take advantage of a special-offer flight and visit somewhere new. Have a takeaway and use disposable plates if the washing-up is really getting to you when the baby's teething. Watch a comedy show and laugh together. Buy some paints and have a go. Grow some vegetables and cook them. Go swimming, climb a mountain, or wander among the antique shops or go clubbing or on retreat together. Keep in touch with your local church.

Healthy, happy marriages are about giving space to one another, so that neither of you feels they can't breathe. Respect one another's space and spend some times with others of your own gender. Give the children some times on their own with one of you as well as full family times, and allow one another times to be on your own, without feeling the other's body language is resentful about that. It's all a question of being aware of one another's needs and erring on the generous rather than the mean in our treatment of one another, even when we know one another really well.

Keep photo albums or boxes of pictures so you can surf the memories from time to time. Make family scrapbooks of holidays, and keep a 'treasure box' of any special cards or letters if you want to – but don't be offended if your partner isn't going to want that kind of thing! Go on being romantic, however many years you're together. A rose or a bunch of violets . . . candlelight . . . cuddles and kisses . . . bathing one another . . . reading to one another . . . special meals . . . sunset walks . . .

'It's the sharing, and the little things I miss,' I was told by a twice-widowed lady who has enjoyed two very special marriages. 'When you've been out somewhere and can come home and talk about it all with your husband over a cup of tea, and know they're really pleased and interested because they love you . . . just the little kindnesses . . . and touch – standing with your arms round each other, or walking holding hands.'

Strong and beautiful marriages grow and blossom not through the occasional expensive event but through those little things my friend was talking about. Simple, really, and lovely because we can all do that, however rich or poor we are. Whether we're in sickness or in health. Whether the circumstances are better or worse. Marriage is the beauty of lives shared in love.

Wedding blessings

If you are getting married at a civic ceremony, you can still have a service of prayer and dedication after the civil marriage, in church or anywhere else for that matter. There are no legal registers to be signed, nor are the banns called, and since the minister or priest is not in this case acting in the role of registrar, the ceremony doesn't have to take place in a registered church building.

For most cases the church itself is the obvious place to have such a service of dedication. Going into the house of God establishes your intention to ask God's blessing as you begin this commitment of marriage, and the service can reflect all the joy and celebration of your wedding.

It's a different service from a wedding, though, and you come in together as man and wife. I think that's important – otherwise the civil service would be robbed of its own solemn and special significance. It's at the civil service that you exchange rings and make your vows.

The dedication service may start with prayer and reflection, recognising our need of God's love and forgiveness. Many couples find this atmosphere a great help, especially if there has been a failed marriage in the background. Those wanting to marry a second time usually believe wholeheartedly in marriage as a lifelong commitment 'for better, for worse'. But sadly things can go badly wrong, and when they do it is God's forgiveness that the church wants to proclaim. Recognising as part of the service that things have gone wrong, but can be forgiven, is a very healing experience.

After a reading or two, the dedication brings the marriage vows before the couple who rededicate themselves to one another.

The rings can be blessed and there can be prayers suitable for the particular circumstances of the family before a final blessing.

This too is very flexible, so as to allow for those families where there may be not only hope and joy but also some hurt and fear among the children. In bringing all this into the service there is an integrity and openness which allows the couple to earth their commitment in God's love and understanding, so they can embark on their new marriage with the past properly addressed and the future free and blessed.

For some, the dream of a heavenly wedding may be to get married under the sky, on the top of a mountain, in a bluebell wood, by a waterfall or lake. Perhaps you feel that such places have a kind of holiness because of their beauty and seclusion.

Although at the present time weddings at such places are not possible, that may change in the future. In the meantime, a service of prayer and dedication can take place outside. Talk to your pastor, minister or priest about it. If they are happy to lead it, they'll work with you on readings and prayers so that the service is gracious and reverent, in keeping with the surroundings.

Here's an 'open air' prayer for you to use:

Great Spirit of God,
your love is wider than the sky above us,
deeper than the sea's depth,
firmer than the strong rock under our feet.
In the beauty of this world,
breathed into being through your love,
N and N have come
to celebrate their love for one another,
to dedicate to you their life together
as husband and wife.

Bless them with the warmth of kindness,
the strength of faithfulness,
the brightness of joy
and the depth of your peace.

Thanksgiving for marriage

I want to include a suggestion for one of those special wedding anniversaries, to celebrate with thankfulness the years you have shared.

Consider going back to the church in which you were married for a short service of thanksgiving and renewal of vows. After a time of prayer and reflection on all the shared experiences of the years together, and a reading, there can be a simple but very moving ceremony, like this one from the Church of England:

Husband and wife face each other and hold hands.

The husband says:
I, *Gordon*, took you, *Audrey*, to be my wife;

The wife says:
I, *Audrey*, took you, *Gordon*, to be my husband;

The couple say together:
to have and to hold from that day forward,
for better, for worse, for richer, for poorer,
in sickness and in health, to love and to cherish,
till death us do part, according to God's holy law,
and this was our solemn vow.
Today, in the presence of our family and friends,
we affirm our continuing commitment to this vow.

The minister asks the congregation:
Will you, the family and friends of *Gordon* and *Audrey*,
continue to support and uphold them
in their marriage now and in the years to come?

All: We will.

New rings can be blessed, or the wedding ring promises renewed, and the service ends with appropriate prayers and the blessing.

It's a lovely way to celebrate. Sometimes couples come with their best man and bridesmaids and a few wedding photos, and it's so special for them to be standing together at the altar, still loving one another.

Other couples may want to renew their vows not because things have been wonderful but because they haven't. If there has been a time of separation or a difficult and painful time in a marriage, and you want to mark a fresh commitment to the marriage vows you made at your wedding, this is a lovely way of doing it.

You may want to return to the church of your wedding, or it may be more appropriate to make a fresh start in the place where you're now living. It can be such a healing experience to voice the regret and the sadness, in God's presence, and allow the weight to be lifted away by God's love and forgiveness, before renewing the vows, one to another.

Churches are not places just for the good times, but for all the reality of life – the aches and tragedies as well as the joyful celebrations. They are Christian communities called to be a focus of what it means to be human; there to listen, support, comfort and encourage through the whole of life.